THE EXTREMELY SERIOUS
GUIDE TO
PARENTHOOD

Being a parent is a life sentence – with no remission for good behaviour.

THE EXTREMELY SERIOUS
GUIDE TO
PARENTHOOD

KEITH RAY

COLUMBUS BOOKS
LONDON

Other books in the *Extremely Serious* series:
The Extremely Serious Guide to Fitness and Health
The Extremely Serious Guide to Sex
The Extremely Serious Guide to Business

Copyright © 1986 Keith Ray
First published in Great Britain in 1986 by
Columbus Books Ltd
19-23 Ludgate Hill, London EC4M 7PD
Designed by Kirby-Sessions, London
Typeset by Falcon Graphic Art Ltd
Wallington, Surrey
Printed and bound by R.J. Acford Ltd
Chichester, Sussex

ISBN 0 86287 214 6

CONTENTS

Preface 6
Introduction 7
The Role of This Book 12
Whom This Book is Aimed At 15
The Prerequisites of Parenthood 17
Training for Parenthood 19
Children's Names 22
The Special Moments of
   Parenthood 25
The Ages of Parenthood 27
Potty-training 31
Landmarks in Growing Up 35
Sentimentality about Childhood 37
Popular Misconceptions about
   Childhood 39
Taking Advantage of Having
   Children 41
Coping with Difficult Situations
   Created by your Children 43
Understanding 'Childspeak' 49
'Parentspeak' 52
Choosing a School for your
   Children 55
Understanding School Reports 59
What Children Should Call
   Their Parents 65
Pocket Money 68
The Foremost Disadvantage of
   Parenthood: Batteries 71
Self-expression 73
Responsibility 75
The Medical and Psychological
   Problems of Parenthood 77
Ways of Remaining Sane as a
   Parent 81
Keeping your Sex Life Alive 83
Family Planning 87
Child Substitutes 91
A Final Word 95

PREFACE

Forget Dr Spock, forget what your parents told you, forget the advice columns. . . if you want to know what having children is really like, read this book. But take care! It might put you off the idea of children for life – which if you already have them could be a problem.

You will need a sense of humour to be able to read this book. In addition, you may find a bottle of gin helps; I certainly needed a sense of humour and a bottle of gin when I wrote it, to help me recollect in tranquillity some of my own moving experiences as a father. But if you find you can laugh at what follows, then you have a good chance of managing to retain your sanity while bringing up your children.

INTRODUCTION

The origins of this book are very clear in my mind. It all started one damp and cold November morning a few years ago. It was a Saturday. I had decided to spend the morning repairing the light fitting in my young son's bedroom. The light fitting had come off worse in an impromptu encounter with Action Man; precisely what Action Man had been doing up on the light fitting, and what action he had been performing at the time to cause the damage, I was never able to discover (although to this day I still think that particular Action Man has a strange, enigmatic smile on his face). I had reached a critical stage in this task, having turned off the electricity to the house and dismantled the light fitting, which left several bare wires protruding from a hole in the ceiling. At that point my wife came upstairs to remind me to repair my son's bike as he would need it that afternoon to cycle round to his friend's.

I therefore abandoned the light-fitting to repair the eighth puncture of the week on my son's BMX. This was a job I detested, since my son always gets punctures in his rear wheel – which means you have to get your hands and clothes covered in grease whilst removing the chain, and to dismantle various other parts of the bike in order to reach the offending tube. Why sharp objects turn a blind eye to front tyres (which are easy to repair), even jumping out of the way, but have a fatal fascination for rear tyres, seeking them out on all possible occasions, is one of those natural mysteries that only the Almighty understands. . . though I bet He doesn't ride a BMX. Anyway, I dismantled the rear end of the bike, and knowing how vital components can easily get lost on a garage floor I carefully placed all the important bits together on a newspaper just by the garage door. Things were going reasonably well.

Just then my small son came rushing out of the house with tears rolling down his cheeks. I put a fatherly arm around his little shoulders and asked what the matter was. It turned out that his favourite toy, a radio-controlled Jeep which had been a Christmas present, had failed a jump off the kitchen table (a jump that the Jeep on the A-Team had managed successfully – and from the top of a five-storey office block, never mind a domestic kitchen table). It was now lying in bits on the kitchen floor. To console him I offered to repair it without delay.

So I abandoned the bike, for which I had abandoned the light fitting, and went into the house, glue in hand. As it turned out, the Jeep was not too badly damaged, and really only needed its bodywork gluing together. I had reached the critical point of this task, with all the broken pieces covered in

'Don't complain . . . it was your idea to buy him the carpentry set.'

glue prior to reassembly, when my wife came rushing into the kitchen with my son's rugby boots in hand. Had I really forgotten to repair the broken stud on his boot, or was I just leaving it to the last minute as I always do? After all, a loose broken stud couldn't really do much damage beyond severing a few arteries and laying bare a shin bone or two. (That is the subtle way in which my wife raises such issues.) And so I abandoned the Jeep, for which I had abandoned the bike, for which I had abandoned the light fitting, and started work on the rugby boots.

Now when *I* was young and played rugby at school, rugby boots were great big heavy things with solid steel studs riveted and welded to the solid one-inch-thick heavy leather soles by super-heroes, and they never needed repairing because they never broke (mind you, the boots were so heavy it was virtually impossible for the average 8-year-old to lift his feet clear of the ground without assistance from an adult; what's more, they required about four hours of cleaning and maintenance every week if they were not to crack). But now rugby boots are more like ballet slippers, made from thin lightweight leather with nylon (yes, *nylon*) studs which screw into the thin synthetic-rubber sole, and when you buy such boots they come with a little spanner which allows you to remove and replace the studs as necessary. Of course, such replacement is not required for many months and so the little spanner gets safely put away – indeed, so safely that you can never find it again. And this is precisely what happened that morning. I spent the next 20 minutes searching everywhere for it, to no avail; only God knew where it was, and He and I didn't seem to be on speaking terms that day. My wife then decided I was wasting too much time, and that I should forget the stud and just take our son off to his rugby match.

So I abandoned the stud, for which I had abandoned the Jeep, for which I had abandoned the light fitting, and went instead to start the car. As I reversed out of the garage, I remembered the bits of BMX which had been on the newspaper by the garage door. Now they were spread down the drive, and some of them were grossly mis-shapen. It was at the height of my panic about the bike, and how I would break the news of the damage to my son, that he came rushing out of the house in tears again. It seems that this time it was all my fault (according to his mother) that he couldn't take a flask of hot soup to the match like all his friends because I still had not switched back on the electricity. However, my wife was ready with a few words of comfort, telling me that I must be the most heartless, self-centred father in the whole wide world to pack my only son off to a rugby match in the freezing cold without a warm drink; would I like him to die of pneumonia or just catch 'flu?

So I abandoned the car, for which I had abandoned the stud, for which I had abandoned the Jeep, for which I had abandoned the BMX, for which I had abandoned the light fitting, and rushed inside to turn on the electricity so that my precious son and heir could have his flask of soup.

Now somewhere along the line the fact that two wires were still protruding, in intimate contact with each other, from the ceiling in my son's bedroom had slipped my mind (just the sort of thing I'm always doing, my wife said later). So instead of soup we got a bright flash, a loud bang, lots of smoke and a lingering smell of burning rubber.

I sat down in the hallway and took stock of the situation. Had I been a woman I would simply have burst into tears, but men don't burst into tears: they simply take stock of situations at such times. The wiring in the house was burned out, my son's light fitting lay in charred pieces on the floor, his BMX was broken, his favourite toy was covered in dried glue and probably beyond repair, he would probably die of pneumonia in the cold owing to lack of sustaining broth, and he was likely to be expelled from the rugby club for maiming his opponents with a broken stud.

All in all, it looked like being a perfectly normal Saturday in our household.

That evening, when the house had gone a bit quieter, and with only about 28 outstanding tasks to complete, I sat down in the candlelit kitchen and reflected on the lot of the average father; well, not so much the average father but me in particular. To assist my thought processes, I poured myself the largest gin and tonic ever seen in the Western world. I estimated that out of the 24 hours the average day reputedly contains (although personally I doubt this figure because my days never seem to be anything like that long), once I had deducted the time spent sleeping/working/travelling/ eating/washing/going to the toilet/nose-picking, etc. 95 per cent of the remaining 'free' time was occupied running around after my son; and of the remaining 5 per cent four of those per cents were spent recovering from the 95 per cent. Only the final 1 per cent was my own time. I reached for my calculator (or rather, groped around for 20 minutes in the candlelight) to work out exactly how many hours this represented, but unfortunately my calculator could not handle enough decimal places to tell me the answer. I estimated that it must amount to about five seconds a day: five seconds when I am the master of my own destiny, a free agent. (One thing I can't understand is the number of people I know with three, four and even five kids who find time to do all sorts of useful things like run Scout and Guide troupes, act as secretary to the local Round Table, organize holidays for disadvantaged children, play in squash and badminton leagues, and accomplish all manner of adventurous DIY projects round the house; and here am I, with just one child, left with a mere five seconds of free time. Maybe people with lots of kids enjoy longer days than I do as a result of some uneven allocation of time resulting from a strange quirk of the Almighty . . .or maybe I'm just no good.) I reached for the gin bottle and broke the world record I had established only five minutes earlier.

I decided there and then that it was my duty to tell all the non-parents around what they would be letting themselves in for if they were to have children. I reached again for the gin bottle but it was by now empty; I had to make do with scotch instead. I resolved that as soon as, or if ever, I was sober enough again I would make a start on a book. Who knows, it might be successful, and if it were then the royalties would help to pay for the re-wiring, the new bike, the new toy Jeep, the new rugby boots and above all the gin. I knew it would take a long time to complete with the amount of spare time I had available.

The next morning, with a head like a well-thumped volley ball and a

'OK, so your friend has kicked a ball into the garden . . .'

mouth like a wallaby's pouch, I groped my way from the bedroom to my study to spend my five free seconds of the day typing. The result was the first word of this book. The other words followed more or less one at a time over the next few years.

So far the book hasn't even paid for the gin. . .

THE ROLE OF THIS BOOK

When the idea for this book was first conceived, it was going to be the standard textbook on parenthood, designed so that new parents could read it from cover to cover and thereby gain a detailed knowledge of all aspects of their new role. It soon became clear that this was quite impractical. Firstly, no new parent that I have ever known has the time or energy to read anything from cover to cover (except perhaps the ingredients label of a can of dried milk powder or a 5-year-old copy of *Country Life* in the doctor's surgery), and secondly I, as a new parent myself, didn't have the time to write it to this specification. Also, even if parents wanted to read it from cover to cover it would probably be impossible as within the first few weeks half the pages would have become stuck together with Marmite, rose-hip syrup or vitamin concentrate, thus ruining any chance of literary continuity. So it quickly changed to being a reference document, divided into short, easily digested sections so that parents, in their few brief moments of peace, could pick it up and consult the section most appropriate to their problem of the day.

Then another drawback occurred to me. If it were to be the standard reference manual it would have to be about 500 pages long, and I didn't have that much time to spare; equally, few new parents would have enough spare cash to be able to buy it, and if they *did* have money to spare they would probably prefer to spend it on something less dull in any case (such as a large flagon of cheap gin, a dirty weekend, or a clean weekend for that matter, even a clean Friday afternoon, or anything to get away from the crushing tedium of parenthood). So the work became instead a short non-standard reference manual with special emphasis on value-for-money and amusement potential. As it turned out the shortness of the final document was a particular advantage. It became small and light enough to carry anywhere, and in particular small enough to slip under a pillow, as it was likely that the only place any parent would get the peace and quiet required to read it would be in bed (in my experience that is about all most parents want to do in bed anyway, as they are generally too shattered to do anything more exciting there).

In spite of these restrictions, however, I felt it was important that the book should meet certain basic requirements:

• it should be rigid enough and heavy enough to be used in the delivery of a firm reinforcement of an ignored or misunderstood request to an offspring's backside.

- the cover should be impervious to Marmite, chewed rusk, orange juice, milk formula, Milton sterilizing fluid, rose-hip syrup and other fluid substances best left unstated.
- it should be thin enough to be torn in half as an aide to relieving parental frustration.
- the pages should be easily tearable and sufficiently absorbent to clear up those little messes that epitomize childhood.
- the book should present an honest, clear and straightforward picture of what parenthood, especially in the early years, is like. However it was decided on reflection that this would be simply too terrifying a document ever to sell, so instead the work is totally misleading, confusing and dishonest; but at least it provides a good read.

Finally I have come to discover that the book has an added side benefit. For people who need one, it is a perfectly safe and almost 100-per-cent effective contraceptive, acceptable even within the Catholic Church; reading a short passage from between these covers every night will ensure that any sane adult will never want to indulge in any activity that could propel him or her into the ranks of that most pitiable section of the human race. . . the parents.

'Call yourself a magistrate! How can I ever show me face again in the gang with a measly fine of £2?'

WHOM THIS BOOK IS AIMED AT

This book (especially in the hardback edition) is often aimed at my young son, since I find it has just the right shape and weight to reinforce otherwise ignored instructions and requests; in other words, it stings without doing any serious or permanent damage. For this purpose I cannot recommend it too highly to any readers who are parents of 8-year-old sons. (For those readers with a serious interest in this function I can send precise throwing instructions, and, under separate cover, good excuses to make to any inquisitive social worker/police constable. Currently I am working on a steel-edged edition for really stubborn children which will be available, by mail order, with especially attractive insurance cover against litigation.)

However, in terms of readership, I had originally aimed the book at the typical non-parent in the belief that it might help him/her to be absolutely sure of the desire to enter the ranks of parenthood before taking any irrevocable action (any reader who is not too sure what these actions are should first buy and read *The Extremely Serious Guide to Sex*, one of this book's companion volumes). At one time I harboured the belief that this book was the ultimate contraceptive, and that reading even one chapter might tempt a non-parent to take a vow of celibacy rather than suffer the experiences described between these covers. Certainly quoting from this book at an inopportune moment can be a passion-killer. But as the book progressed it became clear that the audience really was much wider than I had originally thought, and with the help of my publisher I drew up a list of potential purchasers:

- those people who are not yet parents and wish to decide if they ought to become parents. (To save them the trouble of actually reading the book I can tell them now that they should not.)
- those people who have already become parents and wish to remember why they made the decision. (This book is unlikely to help them as the decision can scarcely have been a rational one.)
- those people who have already become parents but never wanted to, who wish to recall what they lost and have a good cry. (We are currently working on an edition with super-absorbent pages for the benefit of this group.)
- those people who are about to embark on some activity which might result in their becoming parents and want to assess whether it will be worthwhile. The cost of ten minutes' passion should not be underestimated.
- those people who are about to embark on some activity which might result in their becoming parents but want a good excuse for not continuing.
- those people who are going to become parents within the next nine months but are not yet aware of it.

- Charles David Mansell of 43 Fairhurst Gardens, Poole, Dorset who does not yet realize he is on the way to becoming a parent but will receive a rather worrying solicitor's letter in the morning.
- those people who are parents already but are unaware of it – and who ought to know what they've imposed on society.
- anyone who thinks child benefit is money for old rope.
- anyone at a loss to find a single good aspect of celibacy.
- children who want to know what they've done to their parents who used to be normal, well-balanced human beings.
- children who want to know what they *can* do to their parents if they try hard enough.
- anyone with a parenthood fetish.
- anyone who is unable to have children and wishes to see some positive aspects of the situation.
- anyone who has decided to remain childless and wishes to gloat.
- anyone with the price of the book on him/her.
- anyone who can borrow the price of the book from one of his/her children. (One advantage of having children is that it provides you with a fund of people to borrow from; for this reason it is a good idea to have rich children rather than poor children.)
- anyone who wants a good read.
- anyone who wants a bad read.
- anyone who can't read but has a child who is willing to read to him/her.
- anyone who might feel a twinge of sympathy for a poor struggling author who also has an 8-year-old son to tolerate.

'I don't know! Sometimes I wonder if even your father isn't brighter than you.'

THE PREREQUISITES OF PARENTHOOD

'Johnny was happily playing on the bean bag whilst you were shopping.'

Biologically speaking most people are equipped for parenthood. But on top of the basic biological requirement (i.e. an operational and combat-worthy sex organ complete with user manual) there are many other characteristics which are highly desirable features of any prospective parent. These are not particularly rare or demanding criteria; at least 0.0000000001 per cent of the Earth's adult population possesses them (and he lives in Penge but is in fact unmarried, which does not bode well for the future of the human race). Essentially, it is highly desirable that:

either
- You employ a top-class nanny (in which case all that is required in addition to the nanny is money and a spare bedroom, or a very understanding wife);

or
- You have the patience of a saint: no special saint in particular, just one of the upper-decile in the patience stakes. It is interesting to note in this context that very few saints were actually parents, and not all that many were even married, which must mean something. This may possibly explain how they could afford the luxury of being so patient in the first place.
- You have the strength of an ox: in order to carry child, shopping, push-chair, ice creams, etc. whilst simultaneously trying to board a bus/train/aeroplane or similar. The calm temperament of the ox is also likely to be an advantage. In many ways oxen make better parents than their human counterparts, since we find very few juvenile delinquents or football hooligans in the ox world.
- You have the charismatic authority of a judge: the salary of a judge might also come in useful, and the wig and robes would certainly help keep sticky fingers, Marmite, peanut butter, chewed rusk, etc. off your decent clothes.
- You have the wealth of one of the richer kings: without, of course, the financial drain of affairs of state.
- You have the humour of St Rabitude (whoever he is: sounds like a good sort of name for a patron saint of humour).
- You have the resilience of the most resilient Olympic-standard trampoline (or failing that you are just plain stupid).
- You have the diplomacy of one of the more diplomatic United Nations Secretary Generals: but without needing to reside in New York.
- You have the creative flair of Michelangelo without the commitments of a Sistine Chapel commission.
- You have the unquestioning faith of one of the more unquestioning bishops: the spaciousness of the average bishop's palace might also come in handy.
- You have the knowledge of a university professor: plus the advantage of the long holidays.
- You have nerves of high-tensile steel: allied to approximately the same requirements for intellectual stimulation as the average steel ingot.
- You have the self-sufficiency of an Arctic explorer.
- You have the simple needs, and tendencies towards self-denial, of a hermit.
- You have the energy of an Olympic marathon champion.

With these basic prerequisites, plus three arms, four pairs of hands, six pairs of eyes, no ears or nose, and the knowledge of which end of the child to feed, which end to change and which end to smile at, you will be well on the way to adequate, if not exceptional, parenthood.

'Congratulations, Mr Williams, . . . the front row is yours.'

TRAINING FOR PARENTHOOD

No one is really a born parent; we all have to learn to fulfil the many different facets of this important role, which is perhaps the most challenging the majority of us will ever face. As soon as you have your first child, you come to realize that, far from being passive, non-thinking, sweet little bundles, babies are actually supremely cunning, finely tuned timebombs, capable of sleeping like a log all day then waking up promptly at 11 pm as soon as you want to go to sleep and staying awake all night until you start to feel like a half-inflated inner tube; and this will happen every night of the week on the run. By Friday you will start to question the fundamental justification for human existence. The broken night is perhaps the most

'Of course your new friend can go up to your room, dear . . .'

enduring and consistent feature of being a new parent. No one adjusts easily or naturally to this complete absence of sleep; we simply grow used to it.

There are however some simple training routines which may help the prospective parent ease him- or herself into the new role. Some of these are outlined below.

- Training for a disturbed night: go to bed at 12.00 midnight and set the alarm for 1 am; when the alarm goes get up within five seconds, complete ten answers to the *Telegraph* crossword (to check the mental alertness necessary for responsible parental decision-making), sprint to the spare bedroom, pick up a 15-lb bag of potatoes wrapped in a damp towel, gently rock the potatoes backwards and forwards for ten minutes whilst singing a lullaby, then return to bed and set the alarm for 2 am. Repeat this exercise every hour on the hour every night for one year. If you survive this test swap the potatoes for a real baby. If you fail officially adopt the potatoes instead (they'll be cheaper and quieter).

- Training for feeding: mix a panful of weak, runny porridge; put on your best suit, and using a small plastic teaspoon practise spooning the porridge into an inverted milk bottle suspended from the ceiling and swinging freely above your lap. If more than half the porridge ends up on you or the floor you have failed the test and need to practise more. Once you can do it, repeat the test four times a day for six months.

- Training for being left alone with an infant: lock yourself in a small room with only a black and white photograph of an unripe water melon for company; spend the whole day in intelligent conversation with the picture. Repeat for 365 days on the run. If you are still sane at the end of this you may go ahead and become a parent. If you are not sane try becoming a water melon instead.

- Training for bathtime: fill the bath three-quarters full of lukewarm water; put on a blindfold, tie one hand behind your back and practise shampooing the cat. This is a good approximation of the experience of bathing a reluctant baby. To practise bathing the enthusiastic baby use two cats.

- Training for dealing with night-time colic: beg, borrow or steal four 20-watt portable stereo music-centres; sit up all night with the stereos playing the mating cry of four dozen peacocks at full volume, with only a perforated polythene bag full of wet cotton wool for company until your eyelids feel like manhole covers and your nerves are in tatters. Practise for four nights on the run, and then practise for 15 more without a break. Then extend the test for 20 more nights. If you pass this test try it again.

- Training for poverty: for a trial period of just 16 years try living on one-quarter of your normal income. If you succeed you are financially adjusted to parenthood provided you don't expect your children to go on to higher education.

'I think our little grandson is over-tired.'

CHILDREN'S NAMES

'He's got your hair.'

The purpose of a Christian name, or to be more accurate in our rather heathen present-day society, a 'forename' (but this sounds slightly naughty), is quite simple: it is there so that a person can be uniquely identified by the spoken or written word.

In the choice of name parents yield tremendous power. Few things influence a person's life more than his or her name. For instance, if you call your son 'Aubrey Julian Cecil' the chances of his captaining the England rugby team are virtually zero, or if you lumber a daughter with the names

'Roberta Georgia Dereka Davida Paula' don't be surprised if she grows up with a complex about being female. Further general guidelines for choosing names follow:

- take care not to select an unfortunate combination of initials (e.g. Thomas Ian Taylor, or Penelope Elaine Natalie Irene Smith).
- in the case of girls beware of the dangers of consonant/vowel combinations of initials. Brenda Ursula Roberts may very well marry a man whose surname is Maddocks.
- take care to think about abbreviations/mis-spellings/mis-hearings/translations. For instance, not every child wants to end up being called a Dick, James is nearly always shortened to Jim, whilst Clint is always a fairly risky name (especially for a girl).
- take reasonable care to match the name of your offspring's sex and species. Sue for a boy or Derek for a girl will not engender filial respect, whilst Rover, Fido and Dobbin have their own drawbacks.

There are many sources of names from which to choose. They include family tradition, books on names, *Yellow Pages*, dictionaries, market research, TV, novels, pets, Christmas crackers and pop stars. But regardless of the source of the name, they nearly all fit into one or other of a number of categories:

- Traditional: David, John, Peter, Jane, Mary, etc.
- Upper-class: Henry, Caroline, Charles, Diana, Gervase, etc.
- Lower-class: Wayne, Sharon, Darren, Craig, etc. (the so-called 'Escort windscreen' names).
- Flowery: Rose, Rosemary, Iris, Tulip, Daisy, Ragwort, Hemlock, Pond-weed, etc.
- Very traditional: Egbert, Ethelred, Canute, Boadicea, etc.
- Unfashionable: Adolf (especially for girl), Genghis, Idi, etc.
- For children you don't like: Scum, Entrail, Ratbag, Farto, Bogey, etc.
- Historical: Luther, Henry V, Charles II, James I, etc.
- Biblical: Joshua, Noah, Jesus, Faith, Testament, Genesis, Creation.
- Commemorative: Christmas, April, May, Hangover, Goodscrew, Climax.
- Dated: Elvis, Englebert, Ringo, Bing, etc.
- Descriptive: Stump, Wally, Dumbo.
- Normal but trendily spelt: Ppeter, Jjohn, Charlz, Karolyne, ffHenry, etc.
- Pretentious: Duke, Prince, Earl, Pope, Supremo, God, etc.
- Based on holiday destination: Palma, Palermo, Elba, Rochdale, etc.
- Unique: Splanfargenhorst, Moggietrapslobter, Golecktingfowl.

'You wouldn't let me have a dog or a cat . . .'

THE SPECIAL MOMENTS OF PARENTHOOD

There are certain very special moments of parenthood which are familiar to virtually every mother and father, and which will stick in their minds long after the children have grown up and left home; such moments will never be fully understood by the childless amongst us (who may possibly count themselves lucky after reading this section). Some of these magic moments (each of which has been personally experienced by the author within the last year) are described below.

- You are going away to the West Country for the August Bank Holiday weekend and have just spent four hours crawling through heavy traffic to join the M4 westbound. At last you are on the motorway, stuck in the outside lane, making excellent progress at about 2 mph. The weather is typical British bank holiday weather; it is cold and raining heavily. It is starting to get dark. Having just passed a service station, you notice a sign announcing that the next services are 30 miles westward. On the radio you hear advance warning of traffic queues, and at the same time your speed of travel drops to about 1 mph. You are surrounded by fuming, towering juggernauts. At that precise moment your 2-year-old announces that she wants to spend a penny . . .desperately; not in 30 miles time, but *now*!

- You are going out for the evening for the first time in a year. It is your anniversary. You are using a new babysitter who has made it quite clear that she expects the children to be in bed fast asleep before you depart. Your little toddler has been particularly active all day, and you have spent the last two hours walking him to make him tired and then given him a hot bath, a warm drink, two generous teaspoons of Calpol and Phenergan, and spent one hour reading him a bedtime story whilst he snuggles up in his pre-warmed bed. You have also broken all your own rules and made ridiculous promises about trips to the zoo, ice creams, chocolates, and watching television until late the next day *provided* he goes to sleep straight away. He starts to nod off, and you spend the next hour creeping round the house barefoot like a deformed monkey, getting ready to go out; you scarcely dare breathe. As 8.30 pm approaches you hover by the front door so that you may see the babysitter arrive and open the door for her without the risk of her ringing the doorbell. You see the babysitter coming up the drive and open the door in readiness; just as she reaches the door the telephone rings. Your toddler wakes up screaming. End of evening out.

- You have planned a particularly romantic evening. Without your wife realizing, you have chilled a bottle of champagne and smuggled it up to the bedroom, you have lit the candles, you have romantic music playing, a scanty lace nightie is ready for your wife to slip into, or out of, and you have placed a bunch of red roses by her pillow. You go downstairs to invite her to come to bed with you. Touched by the aura of romance, she agrees readily. You lead her upstairs expectantly. When you open the bedroom door you find your 3-year-old sitting up in *your* bed, 150-per-cent awake, with four boxes full of Lego, two Action Men, three teddy bears and his favourite book -- from which he expects to be read another bedtime story. End of romantic evening.

- After a whole weekend without mentioning anything about homework, your 7-year-old is getting his belongings ready for school. You are late that morning and have to leave the house within the next 15 seconds if you are to deposit him and catch your usual train. It is vital that you get to work on time because your company's most important client has arranged a meeting with you prior to signing a £4 million order. Your wife has already left for work. In desperation you grab everything – your son, his briefcase, his rugby boots, your briefcase and your coat – under one arm and rush frantically for the front door. Just as you are on the point of locking it, he calmly announces that he forgot to tell you that he has to take four different 'things to do with spring' to school otherwise he'll get into terrible trouble from his teachers. After spending 5 valuable seconds tearing round the garden pulling up any plant that looks vaguely springlike and cramming it into your offspring's sticky hands, you then drive at 90 mph to the school, scrape another parent's car on the way out, get booked for speeding, miss the train, lose the order and get severely reprimanded by your boss. Your resultant foul mood lasts all day and into the evening, making the domestic atmosphere exceptionally strained. After supper your youngster calmly announces that it was all right at school, because it was *next* week, not this week, that he had to take the spring things into class. Your thoughts turn seriously to the notion of enrolling in the Foreign Legion.

'Don't kid yourself about rearing a childhood prodigy, Dad . . . It's just you who's thick.'

THE AGES OF PARENTHOOD

(as classified by pub-patronage behaviour)

Parenthood goes through many different phases; the most obvious ones are (1) the new parent (all idealistic and starry-eyed); (2) the established parent (concerned primarily with the practicalities of child-rearing, like buying clothes, choosing schools, birthday parties, toys, etc.); (3) the blasé parent (who knows it all after two or three kids and is really getting rather bored by the whole thing); (4) the mature parent (who from a practical point of view is scarcely an active parent at all as his/her children are virtually grown up); and (5) what we might call the nominal parent (parent in name only as the kids have left home). After these stages come successive re-births as grandparents, great-grandparents, etc.

However, this sort of classification of parenthood disguises the fact that there are numerous finely differing sub-phases of being a parent which can be gauged in terms of the effect the presence of offspring has on normal living. With this in mind a new classification of the ages of parenthood is presented below.

AGE OF CHILD	PUB-PATRONIZING CHARACTERISTICS
From verification of pregnancy to birth	Also known as the hangover phase. It is largely because you went to the pub and got drunk, but not too drunk, that you are on the verge of becoming a parent. This may affect your attitude to social drinking for the rest of your life, and could lead to solitary drinking with its attendant lower risk of pregnancy.
Birth to 1 year	You can go to the pub at virtually any time you want once the baby is asleep provided you can stow the carrycot in a quiet corner. Its very presence may serve as a salutary warning to other drinking couples of the dangers of over-indulgence. However, finding a pub that will let you in with a carrycot could be a problem.

1 to 5 years

You can scarcely go to the pub at any time, unless you can persuade someone to babysit, even though you'd give anything to abandon the noise and nappies while you grab a fix of alcoholic oblivion. Also, the chances are you'll be so tired from broken nights that all you'll want to do in the evening is fall asleep.

5 to 8 years

You can go to the pub at any time during school hours or to a pub with a garden, but you won't enjoy it. You'll be spending so much time chasing after the kids that you'll hardly get a chance to drink anything.

8 to 10 years

Although you might get a babysitter, and indeed the kids might be all right left on their own for a while, they'll make you feel like the most uncaring, inconsiderate parents on earth for leaving them alone while you sneak out to enjoy yourselves.

10 to 14 years

The children would love nothing more than to be left alone whilst you go to the pub, but you can't trust them to behave for a minute, and you can't do much drinking in a minute; and in any case your children's lifestyle ensures that you can scarcely afford visits to the pub any more.

14 to 16 years

The children could go with you to the pub and drink quite legally as long as they were having a meal, but going out with you is just about the last thing they want to do. They would never live down their friends' ridicule if they were seen out with you.

16 to 17 years

You could go to the pub any time and probably trust your kids to behave themselves while left on their own. But the chances are you'll run into them having an illicit drink at the pub, which could be embarrassing; so it's better to stay away. (However, if you *did* run into them they could at least give you a lift home on the back of the motorbike.)

17 to 18 years

As with the last age-group you might run into your offspring while out drinking, but now they could drive you home in more comfort – in a car.

18 to 30 years	Your children are now quite good to go to the pub with, and may well buy you a drink. This is about the only age at which it is easy to go to the pub with one's offspring, but the chances are they'll be too busy chatting up the opposite sex to be bothered with you.
30 to 50 years	At this stage your children may well be better able to afford the drinks than you can, but are likely to have young offspring of their own and hence be stuck in one of the categories listed above.
50 to 70 years	By now you may be dependent upon your offspring to push you to the pub in your wheelchair, but the chances are that they'll live too far away.
70 years +	By now you may be too old to go to the pub, but if your offspring are really successful they may be able to buy you a brewery of your very own, thus removing the need to go to pubs.

It is interesting, but rather depressing, to note from the above that it is virtually impossible to make an enjoyable visit to a pub once you have children, even if you have the requisite money and energy.

'Daddy, when will my tummy start to droop like yours?'

'It was one of his earlier portraits.'

POTTY-TRAINING

According to the child psychologists, one of the most important aspects, if not *the* single most important aspect, of bringing up a child is the matter of potty-training. The one thing, they say, that will decide whether your offspring will become prime minister or delinquent, bishop or beast, good family man or pervert, business tycoon or drop-out, is how you teach him to use the potty. Get the potty-training wrong, they say, and you are condemning your child to a lifetime of suffering and deprivation. Get it right and you'll be giving him the equivalent of a silver spoon in the mouth.

To be strictly correct, of course, it is not *potty*-training that needs your attention but child-training; most potties don't need to be trained – they just sit quietly on the floor waiting to be used. It is the child who needs to be taught when and how to use it.

Different parents approach potty-training in different ways. Some take it very seriously and chart progress every day; in extreme cases they may even throw potty-training parties where they share with their (somewhat perplexed) friends and neighbours the joy of that magical occasion when the potty was first used successfully. Other parents take a much more matter-of-fact approach and accomplish the potty-training with scarcely a second thought.

Much argument centres on when potty-training should commence. If you listen to the psychologists you might deduce that there is only one correct moment during a person's whole life when he or she should be placed for the first time on that simple plastic receptacle: place the child on the potty one minute too soon and failure will follow him all his life; leave it one minute too late and the resulting psychological damage will be immeasurable. Other favourite topics for discussion among the child psychologists include the art of persuasion, the technique of persistence, and the question of reward for successful use/punishment for failure. Even the colour of the potty could have psychological overtones, so it should be selected with great care.

Many of the worst mistakes can be easily avoided. Outlined below are some psychologists' views on different aspects of potty-training:

- Potty-training too early: this often results in a bodily function-dominated lifestyle scenario in which the id and the ego are in constant conflict as a result of the parental-praise/natural age-related sphincter control dilemma – a good breeding ground for schizophrenia in later life. It is commonly believed that Van Gogh was potty-trained too early, and that his self-mutilation, prior to his severe schizophrenic symptoms, was triggered by his recognition of this fatal parental error.

- Potty-training too late: this can result in conflict between the natural retrogressive desire to be nappy- (and hence parent-) dependent, and the latent contra-tendency for self-imposed continence experimentation. The unavailability of success/recognition attainment situation scenarios in the pre-potty infant life-stage can lead to self-respect denial and low career ambition in later life: a common cause of social rejection, drug abuse, self-denial and self-inflicted mutilation.

The ideal age for potty-training is believed to be 9 months, 4 days, 3 hours 3 minutes and 12 seconds, with an acceptable tolerance of +25 seconds. A recent study has shown that 65 per cent of murderers were potty-trained at an age more than 2 standard deviations away from the mean age, and that 5 per cent were never potty-trained at all.

- Using a green potty: this can result in the countryside being subconsciously associated with excretory functions. The practice also gives rise to beliefs that rural life is the undesirable by-product of a superior technological city-oriented lifestyle, and to desires to restore the capitalistic ideals of the industrial revolution era. It is believed that the majority of people who litter the countryside were trained on green potties. It is also believed that Brunel, Watt and Stephenson were familiar with green china potties when young, and that this more than anything else led to their conquering the countryside with steam power and railways.

- Using a red potty: this can easily lead to a pathologically excessive subconscious association of communism with human waste and to a fundamental questioning of the socialist ideals of Marx and Engels – whereby the potty may be seen as a training ground for extreme right-wing policies. (Oswald Mosley was frequently placed on a patterned red potty by his nanny before the age of one.) By contrast if the training is completed quickly the reverse effect may occur, with communism being associated with successful human endeavour over physical and mental hardships, as happened with both Mao and Stalin (or Red-Potty as he was known for a long time by the inner circle of the Politbureau).

- Potty-training in too public a place: this leads naturally and directly to subconscious association between anal functions and public recognition, with a consequent low regard for public service.

- Potty-training in too private a place: this, by contrast, engenders guilt feelings about natural functions and is a common cause of sexual impotence, stammering, low self-esteem, etc.

- Using rewards for successful potty use: rewarding an individual for the accomplishment of a bodily function which should come naturally tends to result in laziness and work-shy attitudes in later life; and when the reward is associated with the anal functions success tends to be sought only in the baser areas of life, especially crime.

Clearly, choosing the right conditions for potty-training is paramount. If you choose a potty of the right colour (avoiding red and green), commence training at just the right time (not a second too early or a second too late), in the right place (not too public nor too private), with just the right amount of persuasion and with the potty at precisely the correct temperature, then there is absolutely nothing to worry about.

'Couldn't you have chosen a hamster or gerbil instead?'

'I mixed some dirt and grime into it and then he started eating it.'

LANDMARKS IN GROWING UP

Growing up is of course a continuous process, starting as soon as the child is born and ending (in the case of male children, if my wife is to be believed) somewhere around the age of 45. However, along this continuum there exists a number of landmarks which will remain in the parents' mind for many years, if not forever. Indeed, many parents never tire (although their audience tires very rapidly, especially if it consists of non-parents) of recalling, for example, the first night their infant slept through without a break, or the first time the toddler managed a whole day without a nappy; you can even buy special sorts of diaries for recording every event from the first scream to the first wet dream. This is what parenthood is made of. Some landmarks are common to all children (e.g. the first faltering steps) whilst others are more specialized (e.g. the first bank job, or the first stretch in Parkhurst). Some of the more significant landmarks common to nearly all children are as follows:

- The first unbroken night for the child. This is certainly one of the most significant landmarks, marking as it does the return of the parents to something resembling normal life.
- The first unbroken night for the parents (often coincides with the previous one but may precede it if the parents take drastic action, such as sleeping in the garden, moving to a hotel, or taking five Mogadon each).
- The first unbroken night for the neighbours (in the case of the noisier child).
- The first unbroken night for the local police (in the case of the exceptionally noisy child).
- The first sexual intercourse between the parents after the birth.
- The first solid food eaten by the child.
- The first solid food that stays down long enough to be classed as eaten.
- The first meal at which more food ends up inside the child than lands on the floor.
- The first meal at which the child becomes aware of the immense power he or she can yield by refusing to eat a thing, or eating it and immediately ejecting it on to the floor.
- The first meal at which the child starts to eat more than both parents put together.
- The first attempt by the child at uttering a word.
- The first word uttered by the child that can be understood by the parents.
- The first word uttered by the child that can also be understood by a normal human being (nowadays this can often be as late as the early twenties).
- The first swear word used by the child in full cognition of its meaning.
- The first really dirty word used by the child.

- The first dirty word used by the child that you haven't even heard before and have to look up in the dictionary.
- The first dirty word used by the child that you haven't even heard before and isn't in the dictionary.
- The first interest shown by the child in the opposite sex.
- The first awkward questions posed by the child about sex.
- The first awkward question posed by the child that you don't want to answer.
- The first awkward question posed by the child that you are unable to answer.
- The first awkward question posed by the child which suggests you've been missing out on something all these years.
- The first awkward question posed by the child which suggests that, whilst you may have missed out, your young offspring clearly has not.
- The child's first tooth appears.
- The child's first tooth bites you, leaving a mark that lasts a week.
- The child's first tooth falls out (this occurrence is sometimes a direct result of the previous landmark, with some assistance from the parent's fist).
- The child's first suspicion that the tooth fairy may be one of the people who normally turn up for breakfast.
- The child's first attempt at material gain in exchange for not revealing to a younger brother or sister who the tooth fairy really is.
- The child's first carefully reasoned argument as to why the remuneration for each tooth should be indexed-linked to the average price of a basket of confectionery items in the local corner shop.
- The child's first attempt to raise capital by accelerating natural tooth attrition by artificial means.
- The child's first clean nappy (something parents go into raptures about, even in fairly sober company).
- The child's first nappy-free day (heights of rapture).
- The child's first nappy-free day which turned out to be a mistake (rapture falling somewhat short on height).
- The child's first dry night.
- The child's first wet bed and its associated smell – which lingers for about 15 years on a warm day.
- The first time the child's bedclothes have to be changed more than twice in the same night.
- The child's first unassisted visit to the toilet.
- The child's first unassisted visit to a room which the child *thought* was the toilet but wasn't because you were staying at a friend's house.
- The first time the child asks to go on holiday on his/her own.
- The first time you pray your child will ask to go on holiday on his own.
- The first time you take your child to a respectable restaurant, thinking he is grown up enough.
- The first time you take your child to a respectable restaurant, thinking he is grown up enough but discovering you are mistaken.
- The first time someone thinks your children are your brothers/sisters.
- The first time someone thinks you're their grandfather or grandmother.
- The first time someone thinks you're their grandfather or grandmother and you feel too haggard to dispute it.

And so it goes on. . .

SENTIMENTALITY ABOUT CHILDHOOD

Most parents are, at some time, rather sentimental about their own childhood, often recalling how happy it was in spite of its hardship, poverty and deprivation (hardship, poverty and deprivation which, in most cases, never happened); normally a comparison is made showing how comfortable and fortunate their own children's upbringing has been. Such comparisons usually start with the phrase 'When I was your age. . .' which actually means 'It is so long since I was your age that I can't really remember a thing about it, but I am about to invent a story which should make you feel lucky to be growing up now rather than then'.

The sort of recollections frequently heard are illustrated below:

- When I was your age. . . I never got fancy computerized, battery-powered toys for Christmas; the most I could ever hope for would be the bottom half of a small, fourth-hand, shop-soiled cardboard box which my father would patch up with sticky tape he'd salvaged from the council tip and painted with his own blood. I'd have to share the box with my sixteen brothers and sisters, and at night we'd all sleep in it together to keep warm. And then on Boxing Day he would have to pawn it to get a farthing so that we had half a cold mince pie to share out as a treat for tea. If he had a job and worked really hard, he used to scrape together just enough by the following Christmas to redeem the box to give us again as a present. And that was in a *good* year. We really grew to love that box. We had *real* Christmases in those days.

- When I was your age. . . I didn't get taken to school by car. I had to walk the 25 miles to school barefoot with my shoes tied round my neck so that I didn't wear them out. I used to set out at 2 am come rain or shine to be there by 9 o'clock. And I had to carry my little brother and two little sisters on my back all the way because they had no shoes at all. On the way I used to weave a gross of baskets and make five hundredweight of clothes-pegs to sell to earn enough money for a slice of stale bread to share out between the four of us for lunch; I say 'lunch', but that was all we'd have until the next day.

- When I was your age. . . we could never afford meat on Sundays. Instead, if we'd behaved ourselves during the week, we were allowed as a treat to stand outside the butcher's window looking at the joints of beef. Then the next day we'd shut our eyes and imagine we were eating the beef as we took turns sucking the one boiled potato we had to share between the twelve of us. After we'd each had a suck the potato would go back into the pan for next week. And if one of us actually bit the potato my Father would beat us for sixteen hours with a tree trunk. I still remember the Sunday when my Mother found a bone left by the dog at the big house. . .

• When I was your age. . . my Father worked in the stone quarry from 6 am until 10 pm nine days every week, 58 weeks every year, grinding up solid slabs of granite with his teeth (or rather his gums, as he couldn't afford teeth) to make road stone for one penny a ton. And if the foreman found him without a mouthful of chippings he'd fine him five years' wages, flog him for a month with a sledgehammer and halve his pay forever. And no nonsense about meal breaks: lunch was the smell from the tripe factory washed down with a thimbleful of lukewarm water shared with the other 129 men on the shift. In those days that was enough to keep a strapping lad going for a week. After the quarry he did the night shift from 10 pm to 4 am at the steel mill forging steel ingots between his bare knuckles for a penny farthing a month whilst unpicking old rope with his fingers for an extra farthing a ton. Then it would be straight out of the steel works to spend two hours cleaning out the pig farm, naked in all weathers to keep his clothes clean, before going straight back to the quarry for another day's grind. If he was lucky he'd get a one-hour unpaid holiday every fifth year – and do you know, in 175 years on the job he never had one day off sick except the day he died, and then he was back at the quarry next morning at six. Never once did I hear him complain.

In fact, once we remove the veneer of sentimental exaggeration, most parents' upbringings were really very similar to those of their own children. They just took place 25 years earlier.

'Why were you and Daddy bouncing around in bed so much last night?'

POPULAR MISCONCEPTIONS ABOUT PARENTHOOD

Amongst non-parents (and even amongst some parents), the state of parenthood is surrounded by myth, legend and misconception. Many of these myths are culturally related, and what may be said in one society may not be said in another. However, there are some recurring themes in much of this folklore, and an extensive study in many different countries (well, two to be precise) has produced a list of some of the more important of them:

- Bringing up children gets easier after the first one. This is quite clearly a myth, perhaps based on the fact that when you have more than one child you simply don't have the *time* to notice how difficult it is. In fact if you have more than three children you scarcely have time to think at all, which may be why such people often unthinkingly go on to have a fourth, fifth and even a sixth child.

- Parents enjoy life more. This is, in a sense, partially true; parents actually have very little time (at least during the first sixteen years) they can refer to as 'life' (normally about ten minutes each week), and it is possibly true that owing to their scarcity these fleeting moments are enjoyed more than the corresponding periods amongst non-parents.

- Making love parallel to the Earth's magnetic flux results in male offspring. There is no scientific evidence to support this hypothesis (possibly based on a belief that the magnetic field helps align cells in the formation of the male penis), partly because constantly referring to a compass is a passion-killer. However, whilst it may not result in a boy, it is likely to produce a child with a magnetic personality and iron will.

- Parents live longer than non-parents. This is not true. It just *seems* longer because the time drags.

- Having children makes paying VAT less painful. Again there is absolutely no foundation for this belief, which was possibly started by HM Customs and Excise as a public relations exercise.

- Having children stops you going bald. In fact having children has no physiological impact on the propensity to go bald; however, most parents simply don't have the time to go bald.

- Children respond best to a firm hand. This is not strictly correct. In my experience most children respond even better to a firm foot, firm walking-stick or firm leather strap.

- Men with big feet have intelligent children. This is not true; in fact men with big feet simply produce children with big feet, who may as a result be more stable but not more intelligent. No really intelligent child would ever choose a father with big feet.

- Having kids is bad for the teeth. This is not directly true; although the sexual act which results in kids can, if carried out on a bed which is too close to the wall, lead to impact injuries to the man which can in time loosen the gums' grip on the teeth.

- Having children is expensive. This is definitely not true; having children is absolutely *crippling*.

- A marriage is more likely to survive if there are children. Whilst the real spiritual marriage is no more likely to survive, the actual divorce rate may well be lower; just *you* try finding the time to talk to solicitors with kids around.

- Having kids keeps you young. Not strictly true, although if you have kids you may end up screaming like a 3-year-old much of the time and praying that you were back at school.

- Having children will bring music into your life. This is technically true, although it is not true in the way most people think. In my experience having children does bring Wham!, The Clash, Bad Manners and a host of other groups into your life at around 120 decibels.

(I was going to write another page or so of these myths, but being a father myself I just couldn't find the time.)

'The good news is that I've decided to stop smacking you when you are naughty . . .'

TAKING ADVANTAGE OF HAVING CHILDREN

'I promised Daddy I wouldn't say a word about the watches.'

Although children can be a nuisance and an imposition much of the time, there are certain occasions when having children around can be a positive advantage. Some of the best examples are described below:

● When going through customs with certain items you would prefer the Customs and Excise officers not to see, few ploys can beat having a 2-year-old child around. The secret is to make sure your offspring has had so much to drink on the plane that by the time you reach the customs barrier his or her nappy is absolutely soaked, and that he or she is not wearing any protective waterproof pants. Then, when asked to open your bags, pass the infant over to the officer concerned to hold whilst you search for the keys. Make sure you take at least three minutes to find the keys. In my experience 95 per cent of customs officials do not survive more than the first 90 seconds before handing the child back and telling you to go on your way. It is not wise to use this tactic when the child reaches the age of three because at that age and older he is likely to announce at the top of his voice, 'My Daddy's got four watches in that case' or 'My Daddy told me not to say we have a camera with us'. If the wet-child approach fails to work, for some reason (e.g. the customs officer *likes* having a clammy, wet, smelly uniform), you will need to resort to the ultimate weapon: wait until the officer has opened the first suitcase and has spent at least 30 seconds rummaging around, and then say that you've just remembered you stuffed four soiled nappies into the case just before you left your holiday hotel and you hope he doesn't get his uniform dirty. Watch how quickly his inquisitive hands exit from your luggage.

- If you need, at the very last minute, to cancel a holiday, the best way of getting back your deposit once the normal cancellation date has passed is to tell the travel company that your 2-year-old has contracted a serious illness and cannot be moved. Only the most callous travel representative would refuse the refund or demand a medical certificate.

- Children provide an ideal excuse for an adult to avoid doing all those things he does not want to do: for example, going to the in-laws for a weekend ('Johnny's got mumps'), going to disliked neighbours for lunch ('We've got upset tummies running round the family'), doing jobs around the house ('I can't do it with the children around'), etc.

- Children also provide a good scapegoat in emergencies; for example, when something important gets broken it is much less likely that your husband or wife will get angry if told it was your 1-year-old who did it whilst practising walking.

- If you fancy a day off work children are one of the few excuses that hardly ever provoke any awkward questions. For example, say your 3-year-old fell out of a tree and you had to go to the hospital to have his leg seen to. . .but thank God it wasn't broken, and do you know, you can't even see a scratch from the outside!

- In the event of any person of the opposite sex becoming unwelcomely flirtatious, a chat about your kids, accompanied by photos of them (preferably in the bath, on the potty or exceptionally muddy) is normally sufficient to terminate the interest.

- If you need to see a doctor in an emergency, it is always easier if you arrive at the surgery with an apparently sick or injured child; once the doctor has attended to your offspring (doctors never refuse to see small children), mention that you've been having a bit of back trouble recently and could he possibly have a look at it whilst you're there to save your taking up an appointment during surgery hours when really sick people might need to see him.

- Best of all, children allow parents to act as real martyrs ('I sacrificed everything for my children').

COPING WITH DIFFICULT SITUATIONS CREATED BY YOUR CHILDREN

'I see you've met my pet snake Cyril, Mr Perkins.'

Being totally uninhibited and honest creatures, children have a quite unique ability to put their parents in embarrassing situations. Learning how to cope with these situations, or even profit from them, is one of the most important lessons the new parent has to learn. Much of this learning can only be done the hard way, but a few examples should get the novice parent off to a flying start. Described overleaf are some examples of embarrassing situations taken from real life, followed in each case by the most likely parental reactions. Select the reaction you feel would be closest to your own, then check whether you have chosen the right response from the answers at the end.

SITUATION 1

Your boss has kindly asked you and your wife round for pre-lunch drinks on Christmas Day. He has told you to bring your children because they can play with his own grandchildren and keep them company. All is going well until you are about to leave, when your 3-year-old son comes into the sitting room, pulls down his pants and wees all over the boss's Persian carpet.
  Do you:

(1) pretend he is not your son after all and ask who the horrible urchin is? (The fact that he calls you 'Daddy' makes this particularly challenging.)

(2) quickly step on to the wet spot, hoping the boss doesn't notice, and delay your departure until it has dried out? (This may take several hours and thoroughly drain all your reserves of social chit-chat.)

(3) if the spot is too large to cover by standing on it, faint over the spot and do not come round until it has dried out? (The danger here is that after the first comatose hour lying on the carpet you may be removed to hospital; if so, try to persuade one of the ambulance men, as discreetly as possible, to take over the camouflaging role for you.)

(4) announce loudly that real Persian carpets don't stain so it shouldn't matter?

(5) quickly and discreetly mop it up before anyone notices?

(6) offer to get the carpet professionally cleaned?

(7) buy the carpet for cash on the spot for the price your boss paid, adjusted for inflation plus a margin of 25 per cent (and don't ask for a receipt)?

(8) move rapidly to the other side of the room with your offspring and then enquire loudly whether anyone else saw the dog walk through the room?

(9) ask your boss whether he is still having trouble with his continence problem?

(10) offer your resignation on the spot and then collapse, dead?

  Although options 2 and 3 will conceal the problem, they are time-consuming, whereas 10 is the coward's way out, and few people will have the courage for 4, 8 or 9. The wisest solution is clearly 7.

SITUATION 2

You are waiting to cross the road at a busy junction where the traffic is being controlled by an exceptionally attractive young policewoman. Suddenly your 4-year-old son shakes off your grip, runs halfway across the road to the policewoman and shoves his hand up her skirt.

Do you:

(1) run after him and put your own hand up her skirt to pull your son's hand away?

(2) as above, but see if you can make the policewoman smile at the same time?

(3) turn and run?

(4) calmly walk up to the policewoman and explain that your son has always been fascinated by black tights, to say nothing of frilly white knickers, and by the way is she doing anything tonight?

(5) walk boldly up to the policewoman and announce proudly that the boy takes after his father?

(6) walk up and pull your son away smartly?

(7) shout 'Stop, thief!' and wait for the policewoman to remove her thigh from your son's hand?

(8) shout 'Put her down. . .you don't know where she's been'?

(9) walk up to the policewoman and announce that you'll tell the boy's father about the episode as soon as he's off the critical list and you'll make sure the boy gets a good hiding – despite his haemophilia, brittle bone disease, heart problem and blindness?

(10) ask the policewoman to marry you once you've got a divorce from the little wretch's mother?

In spite of the attractions of 1, 2 and 4, the simplicity of 6 and 8, and the inventiveness of 5 and 9, the most sensible reaction, and the one least likely to get you arrested, must be 3.

SITUATION 3

Your wife has invited your spinsterly neighbour, a pillar of the local church and secretary of the village WI branch, in for coffee one Sunday morning. During a lapse in the conversation your 3-year-old remarks loudly that 'Daddy has a big dark willie'.

Do you:

(1) drop dead?
(2) explain that Willie is actually a tortoise, and he always goes dark just prior to hibernation?
(3) quote statistical evidence to support or deny the allegation about your organ size?
(4) show her so that she can form her own judgement?
(5) say 'I don't think Miss X is interested in big dark willies'?
(6) ask her whether she is interested in big dark willies without jumping to any premature conclusions?
(7) announce that your offspring is very proud of his/her daddy?
(8) distract the visitor's attention by spilling your coffee on the carpet?
(9) distract attention even more effectively by spilling coffee over your visitor?
(10) scream?

This is a tricky one to handle. Probably the only acceptable solution is 1. At least, this course of action ensures that you will not produce any more offspring to embarrass you this way.

SITUATION 4

You are trying to sell your house, and have just finished showing a couple of patently gay men round. As they are about to leave, and whilst they are within earshot, your 6-year-old daughter asks in her piping treble whether they are men or women.

Do you:

(1) say 'No, they're just gays, dear'?

(2) say 'No, they're simply a pair of roaring poufters'?

(3) say 'I'm not sure'?

(4) say 'Of course they're men or women'?

(5) say 'I'm not sure. Just give me a minute to find out'?

(6) belt the kid for all she's worth and say you never really wanted kids because you're a bit bent yourself?

(7) say that you'll give a 10 per cent discount to gays?

(8) collapse on the spot and hope they don't try to give you the kiss of life?

(9) quickly point out how ideally suited the property is to kinky parties?

(10) take the house off the market?

In this tricky situation, where the damage has already been done, the only response likely to retain the buyers' interest will be 7. There can be distinct advantages when selling a house these days to appear potentially bisexual or at least leave doubt in the minds of prospective purchasers about your real preferences. Ideally, however, keep your kids out of the way on such occasions.

SITUATION 5

You have recently moved into a new neighbourhood and have felt obliged to ask the neighbours round for a drink. But you have already taken a deep dislike to one of them. Your 4-year-old marches purposefully up to the individual concerned and announces at the top of her voice, 'My Daddy doesn't like you'.

(1) quickly turn your attention to the furniture and remark, 'No, I've never liked yew; I've always preferred rosewood myself'?

(2) say 'Ewe *can* be tough at this time of year; lamb is so much nicer'?

(3) comment on your child's honest, outgoing personality?

(4) belt the child round the ear?

(5) explain that she has mistaken the neighbour for her detestable Aunt Maud, who visits whenever they let her out of Broadmoor?

(6) say 'Thank God her father's not here today' and apologize?

(7) just apologize?

(8) expand on the reasons why you don't like the neighbour in the hope that your honesty might just be some sort of saving grace?

(9) say 'It's just her little joke'?

(10) make a determined effort to get the neighbour smashed out of her mind in the hope that she won't remember a thing in the morning.

Provided you can think quickly on your feet, either 1 or 2 is the best way out of this tricky situation. Failing that, try 10 – provided there is enough booze in the house. Otherwise be bold and try 6, making sure your dearly beloved child makes a quick exit before she can call you Daddy.

UNDERSTANDING 'CHILDSPEAK'

Although on the face of it most children speak the same language as their parents, they often use words and phrases in subtly different ways. The result is what we call 'childspeak'. Childspeak is a vitally important language for any parent to master, and although an exhaustive exegesis is beyond the scope of this book you will find illustrated below some of the more commonly encountered phrases. Most of these will be familiar to the well-established parent, but the new parent should gain the advantage over his/her offspring by learning the inner meaning of the phrases shown before they are used in earnest against him/her. In each case the phrase used by the child (which varies amazingly little from one child to the next) is followed by a rough translation of what it actually means in adult English. The phrases are divided into those more commonly used by young children and those more commonly used by older children, although there is of course in practice a high degree of overlap between the age-groups.

Younger Children

'I won't do it again'
'I won't do it again until next time.'

'I promise I won't do it again'
'. . . while you're looking.'

'I really promise I won't do it again'
'I won't do it again until the time after next.'

'I really mean it this time'
'I didn't mean it last time and I leave it up to your imagination to decide whether I mean it this time.'

'Goodnight'
'I'll be down again in about five minutes.'

'I'll go to sleep this time'
'I'll wait ten minutes this time before coming down.' (Beware of any child who goes up to bed and stays upstairs without a murmur; he is almost certainly up to no good in his bedroom.)

'I promise I'll go to sleep this time'
'I'll be down again in about ten minutes.'

'I won't come down again, I promise'
'I'll scream for you to come upstairs instead.'

'Are you in a good mood?'
'I've done something naughty and you won't be staying in a good mood much longer.'

'Are you in a very good mood?'
'I've done something *very* naughty.'

49

'I've done something naughty'	'It's best I admit I've been naughty because you'll scarcely believe just how naughty I've really been until I tell you about it.'
'I've done something very naughty'	'Shall I pack my bags now?'
'I didn't mean to'	'I *did* mean to but on reflection I think it was a mistake.'
'You promised'	'You didn't promise, but planting a seed of doubt in your mind might start you thinking you're going senile so you won't deny it.'
'X's dad has bought him a Y'	'Consider yourself a failure as a parent if you don't get me one straight away.'
'X is allowed to do Y'	'X isn't really allowed to, but I want to and I know you'll be too embarrassed to ask X's parents just in case he *is* allowed to.'
'It's been a year since I've been allowed to do Y'	'You let me yesterday and I want to do it again today.'
'If you get me a Y I promise I'll never ever ask for anything ever again'	'. . . not till tomorrow, that is.'
'My tummy aches'	'I don't want to do whatever it is I'm supposed to be doing next.'
'My vision's gone blurred'	'The tummy-ache trick didn't work last time; maybe double vision will get you worried.'
'I've just coughed up some blood'	'I'll manage to put off the terrible moment for at least one minute whilst you go and check.'
'I'm sorry'	'I'm sorry you found out.'
'It wasn't me'	'It was so obviously me I'd better deny it as my opening gambit.'
'Did I do that?'	'I'll just check that there isn't a grain of doubt in your mind that I can capitalize on.'
'I want to do a wee'	'I want to do a wee within the next 1.25 seconds.
'I want to do a pooh'	'I've already done a wee and if you don't stop the car in the next two seconds you'll really regret it.'
'Something's gone wrong with my X'	'I've broken my X.'
'We've been excused homework today'	'We haven't been excused homework but there's something I'd rather do instead and I'll face the music in the morning.'
'Teacher said we're allowed to'	'Teacher didn't say anything of the sort but I know you'd feel too much of a wally to phone the teacher up and check at this time of night.'
'I'll do it in a minute'	'In a minute's time you might have forgotten you asked'; or it can mean 'I'll only spend one minute doing it.'

'I'm full'	'I don't like the meal so I'm going to leave it.'
'I'm hungry'	'I didn't eat the last meal and I know I won't like the next one, so give me a snack now and then I'll have something to blame my loss of appetite on.'
'I'm tired'	'The "I'm full" trick won't work again so I'll plead tiredness and then I can scream for food later.'

Older Children

'Is it all right if I ask a friend round?'	'Is it all right if I ask a couple of dozen friends round?'
'Is it all right if I ask a few friends round?'	'We're going to have a party, and we want to have it here.'
'Are you going out tonight?'	'We don't want you around for the party because we'll all be getting drunk and worse. . .and I wasn't planning to tell you about the party in any case.'
'I won't stay out late'	'You might see me before breakfast.'
'It's one of those feminine problems you wouldn't understand' (said to a father by a daughter)	'I'm going to play my trump card.'
'It's one of those feminine problems you wouldn't understand' (said by a son to a father)	'I'm going to tell you something that'll get you *really* worried.'
'You're being so old-fashioned/fuddy-duddy/square, etc.' (a real thrust to the jugular, this one)	'You're right, but if I capitalize on your vanity there's just a slight chance I might get away with it.'
'If *you* can do it then why can't I?'	'Get out of *that* one if you can.'

It is interesting to reflect that it takes about 20 years to become fully fluent in childspeak, by which time the need to understand it has passed. Hence it is the only language which, once learned, is useless (excepting Latin, perhaps).

'If you want to grow up fit and healthy like me, son, you must eat up your veg.'

'Well, what a pity . . . it's your bedtime.'

'PARENTSPEAK'

In just the same way as children use language in their own special way, so do parents. 'Parentspeak', too, subverts the literal meaning of everyday words and phrases. As a form of language it works quite well until your own children start to understand it, at which point you might legitimately start referring to them as young adults. Some examples of parentspeak are listed opposite alongside their true meanings:

'We know what's best for you'

'We know what's best for *us* and we'll convince you that it's best for *you*, too.'

'I won't tell you again!'

'I won't tell you again until next time I tell you.'

'How many times do I have to ask you to. . .?'

'Just you *dare* tell me how many times I have to ask you.'

'Wait till your father gets home!'

'Give me some time to think of what to do with you'; or, 'I've run out of ideas. Maybe *he'll* have some new ones.'

'That definitely is the *last* time I'll tell you!'

'. . . till next time.'

'When I was your age. . .'

'It was so long ago I can't really remember so I'll make it up.'

'I don't need to take any more of this nonsense from you!'

'There are plenty of other people I can take this sort of nonsense from.'

'I won't take any more of this nonsense from you!'

'I *will* take more of this nonsense from you because I'm at a complete loss as to know how to stop you.'

'If you don't behave. . .!'

'. . . Lord knows what I'll do.'

'It's good for you'

'It's not really bad for you, but I know you'll enjoy it and I don't want you to.'

'Eat up your meal, it'll do you good'

'I don't care if it'll do you good or kill you, but if I've spent an hour cooking it you'll damn well eat it!'

'Go to bed now, you need the sleep'

'Go to bed now, we need a break from you.'

'It's not suitable for children' (of TV)

'You'd enjoy it too much, and besides, we want to watch it in peace.'

'You wouldn't like it' (of food)

'I like it and there isn't really enough to go round.'

'If I were you. . .'

'If I were you I would be doing exactly what you're doing, so stop it.'

'Why do you have to make such a mess?'

'If you dare actually give me a reason I'll crucify you.'

'It'll make you go blind'

'I've run out of rational arguments.'

'When will you start acting your age?'

'I didn't until I was 24, but there's no reason why *you* shouldn't start now.'

'If I'd spoken to *my* parents like you speak to me. . .'

'I *did* speak to my parents like that, which is probably why they kicked me out of the house when I was twelve.'

'You don't know how lucky you are'

'I've exhausted all rational argument, so now I'll try to make you feel guilty.'

'You ought to appreciate the sacrifice we've made'

'I'll make you feel *even more* guilty.'

'If I catch you doing that again . . .'

'If I catch you doing that again I'll be at even more of a loss as to what to do than I am *this* time.'

'It's way past your bedtime'

'We're *desperate* for some peace and quiet.'

'For the *very last time*, goodnight!'

'. . . until the next goodnight in five minutes' time.'

'If you don't behave. . .'
'For God's sake, keep quiet!'

'I expect you'll misbehave.'
'For *my* sake, keep quiet, but maybe God's name carries more weight around here.'

'I must be crazy!'
'How can you be so clumsy?'

'I *am* crazy.'
'How can you possibly take after your father? Doesn't evolution get us *anywhere*?'

'Keep your clothes clean'

'I sometimes pray for miracles.'

'Remember me, Mr Simpkins? I'm the little lad you gave hell to in IIIc.'

CHOOSING A SCHOOL FOR YOUR CHILDREN

'Now *we'll find out why you were sent home early from school with 500 lines.'*

Some of the most important decisions made by parents concern the education of their children, and perhaps foremost amongst these is choosing the right school. In some cases the choice is simple: there is only one school available, and the choice is to send your children there or keep them at home (and possibly end up in prison as a result; with really difficult children this may be an option worth thinking about). In other instances parents are more fortunate and have a range of schools available, but they then face the difficult decision as to which one is best. There is no simple answer to this. Perhaps the best approach is to visit each school in turn and see which one

'My teacher said that if I don't try harder at school I'll end up like you.'

seems best in terms of atmosphere, staff and facilities. Don't be afraid to ask questions, and make a point of seeing some classes in progress. Don't necessarily be put off by old furniture or buildings; it is what goes on in the school that matters, not its fabric or accoutrements. In the end the choice will be a matter of personal preference, but some of the good and bad signs to be on the lookout for are listed below:

Good Signs
Generally speaking, the features listed below suggest a good school:

- The school makes you welcome and someone spends time showing you around.
- You see the headmaster in person.
- The school has a good examination record.
- The children are polite and seem happy.
- The school has good facilities (laboratories, gym, etc.)

Bad Signs
The features listed below generally suggest a bad school:

- You are allowed to view the school only after dark, and someone offers to collect you from home and drive you there (blindfolded).
- You are obliged to remain blindfolded during the visit.
- Someone frisks you before you enter (or worse, frisks you as you leave, or spends most of the time frisking you and clearly gains an unnatural satisfaction from doing so).
- The headmaster will speak to you only through a grille.
- The headmaster has his solicitor present throughout your visit.
- The head will see you only at your house.
- The head offers to see you in bed.
- There is a door inside the school labelled 'Escape Committee'.
- The headmaster drives a Rolls-Royce.
- The caretaker drives a Rolls-Royce.
- The caretaker's gardener's chauffeur drives a Rolls-Royce.
- The school governors all have addresses in Sicily.
- The school governors all have addresses c/o Parkhurst.
- The school has a 'For Sale' sign outside.
- The school is licensed.
- Timetables include such subjects as Hash Cultivation, Drug Dependency for Beginners, Safe-blowing, AIDS Avoidance, Simple Larceny, etc.
- All timetables are written in Russian.
- You are charged an entry fee.
- You are charged an exit fee.
- The school has its own resident probation officer.
- The school is surrounded by an electric fence and pit.
- The headmaster responds to your question 'Do you have a wide curriculum?' by saying 'I'll show you mine if you show me yours, ducky!'
- In response to your queries about exam results, the headmaster asks you what an exam is and where he can get one.
- The head offers you a pint of rough gin in his study before you start your tour.
- The head offers you his secretary before you start the tour.
- The head offers you himself (plus ten used £5 notes) before you start your tour.
- The head asks to see your will before showing you round.
- The head kneels at your feet, whimpering, begging you to send your children there and asking you to name your price.
- The head refers to the children as inmates/economic units/scum.
- The head offers to sell you the school for £25.
- The headmaster dresses in women's clothes, Nazi uniform, or no clothes at all.
- The headmistress smokes a pipe.

'Of course I know the capital of Poland, Mum . . . it's P.'

UNDERSTANDING SCHOOL REPORTS

'So you say the F for English means Fenominal?'

All parents are familiar with that nerve-racking feeling at the end of each term when their offspring bring home their school reports, revealing at last how wicked and lazy they have been that term. School reports are without doubt the most important source of such information, but unfortunately they are not very easy to understand because they are not written in normal English. Instead, teachers use a special form of stylized language which can take some deciphering; and so, for example, if the teacher wishes to tell you that your son or daughter is a nauseating little toe-rag, who's about as popular in school as an incontinent, hyperactive, rabid vampire bat, you'll

'Now you're on to long division your father's not going to be able to help you with your homework any more.'

find the school report describing him or her as 'full of character'. In order to help parents understand what really lies behind these cryptic pronouncements in the school report the following list highlights some of the phrases you may meet together with a rough translation of what they really mean.

'Tries hard'	'Tries hard and fails.'
'Tries very hard'	'Tries hard and fails badly.'
'Could try harder'	'It's impossible to envisage any way in which he could try *less* hard than he does.'
'Good with his hands'	'Useless with everything else.'
'Good manual dexterity'	Exactly the same as above, and is a gentle hint that his future lies in un-skilled manual labour.
'Athletic'	'Not even good with his hands.'

'Mummy said that if I wanted proof that we evolved from apes all I had to do was look at you, Dad.'

'He's got a good head on his shoulders'
'It's a pity there isn't a brain inside to complement it.'

'Stimulating character'
'We have to try hard to think of new superlatives of badness to describe him.'

'Enjoys life'
'He may enjoy life but no one else can whilst he is around.'

'Has settled in well'
'It didn't take him long to realize who's boss.'

'Is settling in'
'He is still finding out who's boss.'

'Is having some trouble settling in'
'We're not yet sure if we'll win in the end or not.'

'Is still a bit unsettled'
'He still thinks *he's* boss.'

'Good average ability'
'Thick.'

'Average ability'
'Very thick.'

'Able'
'He's able to do some things – we just haven't found out what yet.'

'Got potential'
'We may *never* find out.'

'Should go far'
'. . . as far away from this school as possible, we hope.'

'Has a good future ahead of him'
'. . . somewhere else, we hope.'

'Does well when he tries'
'He doesn't try.'

'Sometimes tries hard'
'Even when he tries (which is not often) he still fails.'

'I've got to write a poem about Dad. Do you know a word that rhymes with "wally"?'

'Well liked'	'The other children like him; the teachers hate him.'
'Popular'	'Popular amongst the teachers when he's not at school.'
'A bit of a loner'	'The other kids can't stand him either.'
'Nice cheerful child'	'He's so stupid we can't say anything good about his work, but at least he's harmless enough.'
'Interesting child'	'The same as above, but he's not harmless.'
'Lively'	'Difficult to control.'
'Boisterous'	'Impossible to control.'
'Active'	'Impossible to control even if we could catch him, which we can't.'
'Has difficulty concentrating'	'Both impossible to control and thick with it.'

'If you've got five calculators and you take away three calculators, how many calculators do you have left?'

'Plenty of character'	'Impossible to control and thick with it, but his parents know the headmaster.'
'Full of character'	'Impossible to control but his father is one of the governors.'
'Plenty of spirit'	'He regularly wrecks the place but his father is one of the governors.'
'Full of energy'	'He's always breaking things.'
'Enquiring mind'	'He's always breaking things but is good at making plausible excuses for it, like "I wanted to find out how it works".'
'Breaks things'	'That's about the only thing he *can* do.'
'Creative'	'Always creating a mess.'
'Artistic'	'. . . and the mess usually involves paint.'
'Very artistic'	'. . . it's a lot of paint, normally.'

'A likeable child'	'Surely *some*one must be capable of liking him, because *we're* not.'
'Unlikely to achieve his full potential'	'. . . because we're about to expel him.'
'Overcomes considerable handicaps'	'We don't even like you, his parents.'
'Gifted'	'He can always think of new ways of being naughty.'
'Very gifted'	'We find it quite fun trying to guess how he's going to misbehave next time.'
'Knowledgeable'	'He's never short of an original excuse.'
'Would benefit from individual tuition'	'We beg you to keep him at home and try to teach him yourself.'
'Well behaved'	'You should see the *rest* of the class!'

If a teacher is really at a loss for words to describe your offspring in a form which will not lead to investigation by libel lawyers or the Obscene Publications department, he or she has one final weapon in the arsenal – writing the report in illegible handwriting. It is a very brave parent who asks a teacher what he wrote on a report when the script is totally unintelligible; much better to remain in ignorance and delude yourself that the remarks are favourable rather than find out the truth.

'It was meant to be a sculpture of Mummy, but I dropped it.'

WHAT CHILDREN SHOULD CALL THEIR PARENTS

'What does "transvestite" mean, Mummy?'

To many people the issue of how children address their parents is a vitally important one. Initially most parents get called 'Mama' and 'Dada' – in almost any country in the world, interestingly enough – regardless of the language the child will eventually speak; Mama and Dada are therefore about as close as you can come to natural titles for parents. However there eventually comes a time (normally before the age of 45) when a somewhat more adult form of address is required. The basic requirement is for a form of address which is clear, unambiguous, reasonably discriminating, within the spirit of the Geneva Convention, clean, decent, polite and not too difficult to say. It is desirable in practice that this address takes a verbal form; children could alternatively, in theory at least, be equipped with two dog whistles, one for the mother and another for the father, but this might suggest an inappropriate lack of respect. Often children will ask their parents what they would like to be called; to assist you in making a suitable response to such a question some of the main forms of address have been outlined below; parents should feel free to select the form of address with which they feel most comfortable:

- Normal style: 'Mummy' and 'Daddy' are fairly safe at all ages. Similarly the abbreviated forms 'Mum' and 'Dad' cause little offence (except when directed at the wrong person, such as the milkman).

- Traditional style: the more old-fashioned 'Mother' and 'Father' are equally good, and will suffice throughout the parents' and children's lives. A variant form is 'Mater' and 'Pater'. Much less common is 'Mr X' and 'Mrs X', especially when the family name happens not to be X (a somewhat rare name in any case).

- Energy-saving style: 'Ma' and 'Pa' save about 50 per cent of the energy consumed in saying 'Mummy' and 'Daddy' and are equally acceptable to most parents. 'M' and 'P' save even more energy, but take some getting used to.

- Anti-sexist style: 'Parent' and 'Parent', 'Dummy' and 'Maddy', 'Thing' and 'Thing', etc. avoid possible accusations of any sexist bias implicit in more traditional forms of address.

- Sexist style: 'Father' and 'Father', or 'Mother' and 'Mother', suggest a clear sexual bias towards the parents but at least keep one of them happy.

- Trendy and smart style: calling parents by their Christian names.

- Trendy and not-so-smart style: calling parents by the wrong Christian names.

- Bureaucratic style: addressing parents by their National Insurance or VAT Registration numbers.

- Formal style: 'Sir' or 'Madam'.

- Formal and impersonal style: using 'Sir/Madam' for both.

- Very impersonal and insensitive style: 'To whom it may concern', or 'To the occupier,' etc.

- Exceptionally impersonal: addressing parents only by means of written memos, telexes or affidavits.

- Low-key style: 'Ugh' and 'Mmm'.

- Familiar style: 'Squire', 'Me ol' duck', 'Tosh', 'Mate', 'Watcha, John', etc.

- Purely generic style: calling parents, regardless of their real names, 'Bruce' and 'Sheila', 'Peter' and 'Jane', 'Darby' and 'Joan', 'Abbot' and 'Costello' or some other standard pair of names.

- Technical style: 'Male Parental Entity' and 'Female Parental Entity'.

- The 'I'm-not-too-sure-about-my-real-origin' style: 'Mother' and 'Mother's husband'.

- Friendly insulting style: 'Old boiler', 'Pot belly', 'Old thing', 'Toe-rag', etc.

- Less friendly insulting style: referring to parents as 'Crap-bag', 'Wart face', 'Maggot', 'Pus', 'Boil', 'Nazi scum', 'Worm-infested dungheap', etc.

- Impolite style: 'Hey, you!' for both parents.

- Proxy style: calling both parents 'Proxy!'

- Biblical style: calling the father 'John son of Albert son of Richard son of Henry son of Samuel son of Peter son of David. . .' and the mother nothing.

- Modest style: calling the father 'Progenitrix of the Great Wise One' and the mother 'Progenitress of His Supreme Presence'.

'When I said "How many times do I have to ask you to behave?" I was not expecting the answer "45"!'

'Well, son, it looks like a choice between a birdie three and next week's pocket money.'

POCKET MONEY

Pocket money is one of the subjects that many parents worry about quite unnecessarily; they worry about how much they should give, at what age their children should start to receive it, whether it should be earned or just given, and whether, as parents, they should in any way restrict what it is spent on. In fact the answers to most of these questions are quite straightforward. Some simple but practical advice appears opposite for readers who are not sure what they should do.

- Don't put too many conditions on how pocket money is used. It is meant to be money for the child to spend him- or herself. However, if you do impose conditions, they should be clearly stated and patently reasonable; for example, in the case of an 8-year-old boy it is not unreasonable to say that pocket money should not go on rough gin, vasectomies, fast cars, fast women, face-lifts or gambling. Also, once the conditions have been set, avoid getting into arguments about their detailed interpretation (for example, how fast does a woman have to be in order to be classed as a fast woman, or exactly how rough is rough gin, etc.: this sort of conversation should not be conducted between an 8-year-old and his parents).

- It is o.k. to use pocket money as a reward, but the rewarded task should be one that is reasonable to reward, not one that may be taken for granted (e.g. sleeping, breathing, blood circulation, perspiring, etc.) or one that is unreasonably difficult to attain (e.g. solving the entire National Debt, mapping the surface of Venus, refuting the Law of Gravity, understanding a British Rail timetable, etc.).

- The child should be allowed to use the money for little luxuries if he is to appreciate it. To expect a child to buy his own food from you at mealtimes, or pay his or her share of the rates, or pay for inhaled air on a cubic-metre basis, for example, is not a recommended use for pocket money.

- The amount given should represent a reasonable reward for the effort put in. Avoid under-rewarding (e.g. 2p to a 5-year-old for digging the garden, washing the car, fixing you up with loose women every night, reorganizing your share portfolio and completing your tax return for you) and over-rewarding (e.g. £125 per toy for tidying up his or her room). Suspect over-reward when your children are able to raise a larger mortgage than you can and on better terms. Over-reward prevents the child from acquiring an appreciation of the real value of money.

- Give the money personally; it will not have the same effect if awarded by your accountant, solicitor or bank manager, or if left in a plain brown envelope behind the left-luggage lockers at Victoria Station. Don't insist that your child grovels on all fours for the money.

- It is best if the pocket money is paid in cash, and ideally in coin rather than notes. Avoid cheques, bank drafts, share options, Treasury Bills, loose women, gold bullion, tin futures, Krugerrands or paying the money into a Swiss bank account, etc., even if these actually have a higher redemption value; as far as the child is concerned, they are less negotiable at the sweetshop, therefore less desirable.

- Don't ask for change or a receipt, and don't deduct VAT or National Insurance (unless the pocket money exceeds £35,000 per annum). If your child insists on a properly laid-out payslip he or she is either a budding tycoon or up to no good.

- It is sensible to start giving some sort of pocket money by the time the child reaches the age of five; however, it may be rather humiliating if you are still giving it once your children have attained the age of 65. By this age the state pension should have taken over.

- Make sure your children keep their pocket money in a sensible place. The pocket is not a sensible place for pocket money to be kept. Banks are good places in terms of safety but not as accessible as they might be from the child's standpoint. Piggy banks are one solution, but real pigs are neither very accessible nor very safe, since unlike banks they can run away; but they are more cuddly than real banks.

'Little Jamie's been so happy playing with his carpentry set all afternoon.'

THE FOREMOST DISADVANTAGE OF PARENTHOOD: BATTERIES

This may seem a strange heading for a section in a book on parenthood, but in my experience there is no pronouncement more likely to strike fear into the heart of a parent than the simple word 'battery'. Indeed I have personally witnessed a grown man, a good 37 years old and of significant professional standing, reduced to a quivering mass of uncontrollable human jelly at the statement 'the batteries have run down *again*, Dad' . . . I was that man.

One day shortly after Christmas (and incidentally, my son has his birthday just a week before Christmas, which does not help one bit) I sat in my son's room and placed on the floor all the toys in his possession that require batteries; the total number of batteries required to keep my son's playthings going was 63 – 63 batteries at an average cost of 30p, making a total of £18.90, and each with an expected life of little more than a day. This sober fact jolted me into recording my thoughts about parenthood and batteries for posterity.

- The only people who are *really* deliriously happy at Christmas-time are battery-manufacturers, or people with major shareholdings in battery companies, or people who have battery-makers as relatives or friends. Tell me, when did you last hear of a battery company going out of business? Never! They never do. Battery-manufacturers enjoy a stability of a sort shared only by the Bank of England or the Church of Rome (indeed, I have heard it suggested that the Three Kings actually brought the infant Christ presents of gold, frankincense and alkaline Duracells).

- The gift (to their offspring) most dreaded by parents at Christmas is the toy juggernaut, which weighs about 15 kilos, has working lights, crane and winch, power steering, four forward gears, four-wheel drive, cabin heater, horn, ejector seat, indoor swimming-pool, pool table, cooker, full air-conditioning and fourteen multi-colour searchlights . . . and the phrase 'batteries not included' printed on the box.

- In 90 per cent of cases the batteries cost at least as much as the toy itself, and need to be at 99.999 per cent of their peak performance in order to propel the toy satisfactorily.

- The appeal of the toy to the child is directly proportional to the rate at which it uses batteries.

- You get so used to toys being sold without batteries that when you want to make a special impact on Christmas morning, and buy all the batteries you need beforehand, you find when your offspring unwraps the present that it already has batteries inside. This is the *only* time when you'll find batteries that run happily for years. You'll never need the replacements for which you forked out five quid!

- Even Cindy dolls need batteries nowadays, for their accessories.

- By the time you've realized that rechargeable batteries might in the long run be a good idea (normally Boxing Day morning) you'll find you cannot buy them for love or money.

- When eventually you do get rechargeables (at about £5 a time) and a charger (at about £19.00), on the basis that you'd only need to get new batteries 50 times to cover the cost, your children will have gone right off battery toys and returned to tinkering with Lego.

- When the batteries start getting low you'll find your offspring start switching them around, so that you can never tell which are the good ones and which are the bad ones. That's when you spend an extra £12.00 on a battery-tester.

- When I was young, most toys were clockwork-powered and lasted at least 25 years. Now, when mankind can put a man on the moon (probably a father trying to escape from the words 'Batteries not included'), send a satellite to photograph Neptune (no doubt to see whether batteries are cheaper there), fly passengers at supersonic speed round the word (hunting for the best bargains in batteries,) and can build laser guns which can destroy an enemy missile at a range of 200 miles, the greatest advance the toy-manufacturers can offer is the zinc-carbon battery; why can't toys be nuclear-powered, or propelled by thought waves, or solar-powered, or telepathy-powered or fuel-cell-powered, or ANYTHING but battery-powered?

'Perhaps that'll teach you not to leave your roller skates lying around . . . now you'll miss Blue Peter.*'*

SELF-EXPRESSION

'I hope you're satisfied . . . the karate lessons were your idea!'

At some time all children get into mischief and do something naughty. In the good old days they were simply given a good hiding, a whack on the backside, and they soon came back into line. However, it is now unfashionable to think that children can actually be naughty; instead they are simply 'expressing themselves'. This provides the perfect defence for almost any excess of behaviour. Examples are given below:

- Your young son cuts your father-in-law's best jacket into shreds. He is not being naughty, he is simply demonstrating his early appreciation of the futility of sentimental attachment to material things which is at the core of the collapse of industrial relations in the traditional private-sector industries.

- Your 2-year-old toddler draws a picture on your off-white bedroom carpet using lipstick. She is not being naughty, she is simply manifesting early symptoms of creative textural art-form appreciation.

- Your 4-year-old digs up all your daffodil bulbs. He too is not being naughty, he is simply exhibiting a healthy natural curiosity about the latent symbiotic relationship between man and his environment.

- Your 3-year-old calmly picks up his dinner-plate and inverts it so that his meal falls on to your dining-room carpet. He is not being naughty, he is just fascinated by the nature of the gravitational force fields inherent in the universe.

- Your 4-year-old quietly pulls down his trousers and wees on the floor in front of visitors. This is not naughtiness, simply a manifestation of his appreciation of the value of freedom of human expression initiated by a latent frustration with the capitalistic profiteering motive inherent in the floor-covering industry.

- Your 5-year-old throws a brick through your neighbour's greenhouse. This is not naughtiness, just a demonstration against man's self-gratifying exploitation of defenceless sub-tropical plants.

- Your 6-year-old pours a full can of old engine oil over the windscreen of your car just as you are about to set off for work. He is simply expressing his fascination with the interaction between the contrasting physical properties of liquids and solids.

In similar situations it is easy to think up 'self-expression' excuses for your child's behaviour in order to justify your unwillingness to suppress his or her natural development. Alternatively, you can knock hell out of the revolting little brat to make sure it never happens again.

'It says, "Why not get your window fixed in Bob-a-job Week?"'

RESPONSIBILITY

One of the major tasks of parenthood is teaching children a sense of responsibility so that they can gradually take control of their own lives. The usual way of doing this is to allow the child an increasing degree of responsibility as he gets older until, at about the age of 18, he can assume his full adult role. The difficult task is deciding which element of responsibility is appropriate to each age. As a simple test the reader should attempt to judge the correct age at which a child should be allowed to decide:

(1)   when to go to the toilet;
(2)   what to wear;
(3)   what to eat;
(4)   who to eat;
(5)   which nostril to breathe through;
(6)   whether to breathe at all;
(7)   whether or not to fart in public;
(8)   when to go to bed;
(9)   who to go to bed with;
(10)   how much to pay her;
(11)   how to resolve the US trade deficit;
(12)   where the next major earthquake will be;
(13)   what colour of executive jet to buy next;
(14)   what the meaning of life is.

If you thought age four was correct for all these decisions except no. 2 then you probably have rather high expectations of your children. If you thought none of the decisions was appropriate until the age of 45 then you are amongst the more repressive of parents. If Mummy wouldn't let you answer yourself it is likely that your parents were rather repressive. If you were too engrossed in waiting for permission to go to the toilet to answer the questions then it is likely that you are not really ready for parenthood. If you actually had to make all these decisions on the day you read this book then perhaps you can't really afford the time to read it, whilst if you faced all the decisions but failed to make your mind up about nos. 5 or 6 you are probably now dead and need make no more decisions except, perhaps, how quickly to rot.

'*I've not been naughty, Daddy . . . I've just been manifesting the preliminary symptoms of a behavioural maladjustment syndrome.*'

THE MEDICAL AND PSYCHOLOGICAL PROBLEMS OF PARENTHOOD

There are many medical problems to which parents are particularly susceptible. Indeed, from a medical standpoint parenthood is an especially hazardous phase of life. The more common parental complaints include:

- In-growing toenails; usually the result of constantly treading on pieces of Lego left all over the floor by your dearly beloved offspring. In time this can lead to the Lego-induced bunion familiar to most GPs.

- Sore throat; the result of shouting 'Put that damned Lego away!' every evening for five years.

- In-growing vocal cords; the result of shouting 'Put that damned Lego away!' just once too often.

- Short sight; often caused by spending long hours groping around on the floor, under tables and chairs, in poor artificial light looking for the damned Lego that your offspring didn't put away in spite of your screaming, sore throat and in-growing vocal cords.

- Headaches; in many cases the result of tripping over the one piece of Lego you didn't find in the dark because of your Lego-induced short sight, and then banging your head on a sharp object.

- Amnesia; a common by-product of banging your head too many times after tripping over the Lego you failed to find because of your short sight resulting from groping around in the dark looking for the damned Lego your offspring didn't put away in spite of your screaming, sore throat and in-growing vocal cords. (The advantage of this complaint is that you may well forget what Lego is and where it should go. The disadvantage is that you will bang your head even more often and turn into a sad case of a Lego-drunk parent.)

- Sterility/impotence/torsion of the testes (fathers only); the many possible consequences of failing to notice that your offspring *had* tidied up the Lego, but had put half of it into your underpants.

- Housemaid's knee; commonly caused by crawling around looking for bits of Lego and then accidentally kneeling on one of the smaller, sharper pieces (often to the accompaniment of comments such as 'Oh dear, how singularly provoking' or 'Oh my, what a nuisance!').

- Leg ulcer (or, as it is known technically, Lego ulcer); often the result of repeated Lego damage to the skin and blood vessels in the leg.

- Heart-failure; often the result of discovering just how much the Lego that is spread over the floor actually cost.

- Ruptured tonsils; in many cases the result of accidentally swallowing pieces of Lego which your beloved offspring has concealed inside the food on your dinner-plate (as a present, of course, so that you cannot become angry).

- Indigestion; the result of not catching the swallowed Lego before it ruptures your tonsils.

- Earache; the likely result of the last complaint, combined with the amnesia caused by the Lego-induced head-banging, which itself tends to result in the Lego being eaten in some very strange ways.

- Nasal congestion; caused by having Lego stuffed up your nostrils early in the morning by an enthusiastic (but not medically knowledgeable) 3-year-old.

- Megalomania; the psychological result of the sense of power experienced when ordering your children to put the Lego away.

- Megalegomania; occurring when the *only* thing your children will do when you ask is put Lego away.

- Infantile paralysis; what is likely to happen to your offspring if the Lego-induced damage continues.

- Stress; a common result of worrying about what sort of Lego-induced complaint you'll suffer from next.

- Claustrophobia; the dread of being in an enclosed space in which you are constantly tripping over Lego.

- Agoraphobia; the fear that the Lego might even pursue you out of doors on to the patio or into the grass where the Flymo will transform it into near-lethal shreds of razor-sharp plastic.

- Schizophrenia; with this condition you can't decide whether the Lego-induced claustrophobia or the Lego-induced agoraphobia is worse.

- Persecution complex; you will know you are experiencing this disorder when you finally come to believe that the Lego-manufacturers have it in for *you* personally.

- Manic depression: the psychological effect manifesting itself as a mania of experiencing too many Lego-shaped depressions on the body.

- Identity crisis; when, in despair, you scream, 'Can that really be *my* child?!'

'*Where* has *your father gone to? He'll try anything to get out of playing cricket with you.*'

'What's happened to the manners I taught you, lad? . . . Walking off without so much as a "May I leave the table?"!!'

WAYS OF REMAINING SANE AS A PARENT

There is little doubt that parenthood can be a stressful and trying time for anybody (and particularly during the first 18 years). It is therefore important for parents to find ways of relieving this stress before it reaches dangerous levels (alternatively, of course, they can give in to the stress and become happily loonie). There are many ways of doing this, and each parent should find the method that suits him/her best. Amongst the more common techniques are:

- Writing silly books on parenthood in the vain hope that some wallies will be daft enough to buy them, so that you can at least be a rich loonie rather than just an ordinary one.

- Constantly reminding yourself that it is only likely to last for a quarter of a century or so. This can be done by writing large signs to that effect and sticking them all over the house, or by simply chanting 'It will only last a quarter of a century or so' to yourself for about 25 years. This has the added advantage of ensuring that your own children, disturbed by living with a head-case, will leave home as soon as possible themselves.

- Consuming alcoholic drink, or pouring it down your children's throats (strangely enough, after either party has consumed a bottle of cheap gin the problems of stress suddenly vanish completely).

- Undergoing full frontal lobotomy. In itself this does nothing to relieve the stress (although you might forget what actually caused it), but the stay in hospital should be quite relaxing. After the lobotomy you can always indulge in a few amputations to prolong the stay.

- Absorbing yourself in challenging hobbies such as hang-gliding, free-fall parachute-jumping, bobsleigh, completing VAT forms, etc.

- Taking drugs (especially the narcotic ones).

- Getting away on holiday alone – for 51 weeks each year.

- Employing a live-in psychiatrist. This doesn't help directly, but you can always ask the psychiatrist to babysit. Also, your own exclusive psychiatrist can be a great status symbol, which in itself can be an effective morale-booster.

- Exchanging experiences with other parents (this allows you to go crazy in groups rather than on your own).

- Screaming things like 'Oh, dearie me, how singularly inappropriate that I find myself in the familiar stressed-parent syndrome scenario', or 'Oh shit!'

- Smashing things up.

- Seeking professional help (e.g. nanny, mother's help, *au pair*, cheap tart, etc.).

- Moving to a different address from that of your children.

- Joining the Foreign Legion, British Leyland Fan Club, or some other rare and exotic organization.

- Swapping your kids for someone else's so that you can blame someone else for the state you get yourself into.

- Emigrating without telling your kids.

'Why did you have to go and mess up his lovely elephant trap?'

KEEPING YOUR SEX LIFE ALIVE

Sex is what leads to children in the first place, but once they have arrived it can be amazingly difficult to keep any sort of sexual relationship going, at least with your original partner. Indeed, it is a miracle that so many couples manage to have more than one offspring. Every parent will know that special moment when, tucked up in bed with one's spouse at the height of passion, the whole world just a blur in the background, all human passion concentrated on that magical instant of orgasmic delight, a little face pops round the door and asks you why you are changing sides in bed.

Having a 4-year-old walk into the room at the wrong moment is the most potent passion-killer known to man. On such occasions there is virtually nothing you can do (short of murder or instant emigration) which will allow you to restore the passionate moment and continue the sexual activity to a satisfactory conclusion. After the first hour of lying motionless in bed, waiting for your little child's breathing to return to the pattern of deep sleep, it is hard to think of anything more passionate to do than making a cup of tea or decorating the ceiling.

This is not to say that sex cannot continue after the first child has arrived on the scene; it is just that the expectations and technique may have to be modified. Some of the methods for combining a loving sexual relationship and parenthood are outlined below:

- Make love more quickly than before. If you can manage the whole act from beginning to end in less than 25 seconds there is a reasonable chance of remaining undisturbed. Of course, you will trade off a certain degree of quality and satisfaction in exchange for the opportunity, but the alternative is leisurely celibacy. And making love really quickly can be excellent exercise and quite a challenge in itself to more sporting types.

- Make love at different times – for example, at three in the morning. This may make you feel and look rather like a prematurely senile punch-drunk armadillo in the morning, but at least you'll be a satisfied prematurely senile punch-drunk armadillo.

- Take special precautions to give yourselves sufficient early warning of infantile intrusion to allow you time to make a tactical retreat. To this end, nothing can beat a few squeaky floorboards and stiff, groaning hinges, although an ultra-sonic motion-detector on the landing linked to a siren on the bed-head is a good if rather expensive (and unsubtle) second-best.

- Lock the bedroom door and resist all 'Please let me in' entreaties. This in itself can prove rather challenging to male potency if the crying and pleading extend beyond two hours.

- Make love very discreetly; for example, over breakfast in such a way that no one else at the table notices. The larger morning newspapers can come in very useful on such occasions; at all costs avoid the tabloids. This approach demands a great degree of imagination which can, in itself, prove quite stimulating.

- Take turns at making love to yourself or to the bed whilst your partner babysits. This is certainly less appealing than the other methods, although you can grow to like it in time. It may result in both partners becoming rather withdrawn and introspective, and in extreme cases partners have been known to start fancying the bed more than their spouse.

- Just expect less from your sex life; for example, make love only once a year when your child is so engrossed in his Christmas presents that he won't even notice. For really passionate and really frustrated people this could be extended to twice a year if the child's birthday is included.

- Go somewhere else to indulge your passion. For example, book a babysitter for the evening and check into a cheap hotel; or, if money is really at a premium, just go into your garage and make love in the car. (If it is too cold for this, just dive into a cupboard instead; and if your spouse does not fancy this arrangement there is always the babysitter instead.)

- Get your children involved in lots of activities outside the home, such as rugby, Scouts, horse-riding, etc. This should allow you some private time during the day when you should be safe. But take care; if it is raining heavily indulge your passion with care otherwise you will end up explaining to your rained-off rugby-playing son why you and Mummy had to go back to bed in the middle of the day.

- Become less ambitious and learn to appreciate voyeurism, hand-holding, stroking, etc., which can be done with other people in the room. However, this can have unfortunate long-term consequences; in extreme cases people deprived of normal sex can become so highly sensitized to erotic situations that even a soap-powder advertisement can bring on an orgasm. (In itself this may not cause any great harm but it may result in excessive expenditure on washing powder.)

'I thought I'd told you months ago!'

'Mum's just given me £1 not to tell you something.'

FAMILY PLANNING

A very important element of parenthood is family planning. Strictly speaking this is a misnomer, because it is really more concerned with family avoidance or un-family planning. The purpose is to limit the size of the family so that you don't become totally overrun by kids; normally people want either no children at all or a small, finite number. In theory a woman with a fertile life of about 30–35 years could achieve a total or more than 43 gestations producing at least 43 children, not allowing for multiple births (although she might start to forget what her feet look like). However, the human family is, in practice, almost self-limiting around the four-child level; just try having four children and then see whether you ever get the time, energy and privacy to do anything which might result in a fifth child. It's a miracle that people ever have more than four kids. The average family comprises 2.2 children (although I personally doubt this as I have never seen even one family with 2.2 kids), but it must be said that there are advantages in having a larger family:

- they can save you money, in the sense that you'll rarely get any opportunity to go out and spend what you do have;
- they can offer economies of scale;
- they provide an ideal excuse for going completely round the bend;
- after a while they become self-babysitting, in that the eldest child can supervise his or her younger brothers and sisters for you;
- you are unlikely to be lonely at any time;
- they help save on the heating bills (one child is equivalent to a 1-kilowatt electric fire: with ten kids in the house you'll be needing to open the windows to stay cool on even the frostiest winter day);
- they provide genetic strength for your characteristics: in other words if you have a large nose, ginger hair and a congenital wart on your right ear-lobe, then having lots of kids will help ensure that large-nosed, ginger-haired, wart-eared humans will become the norm;
- you are more likely to become a grandparent;
- you'll get more child benefit (if you ever have time to collect it);
- you'll have more chance of having someone to leave money to, although you'll actually have less chance of having any to leave;
- you'll find it easier to cut up a pizza into four, six or eight pieces than you will to divide it into three;
- you'll nearly always find someone in a good mood;
- if you take a masochistic delight in picking Lego up off the floor, or in reading school reports, you'll enjoy life more with a big family.

However, if you should decide not to have a naturally large family you'll need to find some way of limiting family size. Basically there are three ways of achieving this: by making sex unproductive, by making sex undesirable or unlikely, or by making sex difficult or impossible.

(1) To make sex unproductive:
- use contraceptives;
- mate with the wrong sex;
- mate with the wrong species;
- make love to inanimate objects such as a Porsche 911, an ice cream or the tear ducts or any available part of the endocrine system;
- have a vasectomy or hysterectomy, as the case may be;
- use coitus interruptus (the well-known commercial break method);
- use coitus obstructus (e.g. obstruct all available points of entry with newspaper);
- wait until both of you are over eighty before having sex.

(2) To make sex undesirable or unlikely:
- never wash;
- wear 'AIDS symptom of the day' underwear;
- develop strange habits such as wearing rubber underwear;
- whisper not-so-sweet nothings into your partner's ear, such as 'Am I as good as the first XV?', or 'There's no need to worry, the doctor assured me it's not contagious any more';
- drool and slobber all over your partner;
- become gay;
- confess to having a deeply meaningful relationship with a sheep;

'I think you've got Egyptian 'flu . . . you're going to become a mummy.'

- live on a Boeing 747 (this makes most things, including air travel, undesirable).

(3) To make sex difficult or impossible:
- live with your mother-in-law;
- go to bed wearing armour;
- hang a rates demand or income tax return above your bed;
- make love (or try to) in front of an invited audience of sports commentators;
- join a celibate order of monks;
- indulge in sex only when there's W in the month;
- drink a bottle of gin as a nightcap;
- sell your house and move into a Mini Metro.

Aided by the selection of family-controlling techniques listed above, there can be little reason for any couple to have more children than they really want.

'Oh, dearie me . . . How careless! I've gone and accidentally stepped on his toy trumpet.'

CHILD SUBSTITUTES

If you can't have children of your own, or if your children have left home and you miss them, or if you have children but have forgotten where you put them, or if you can't be bothered to wait the nine months required to have a child of your own, you may find yourself in the market for some form of child substitute. Child substitutes can take many forms, ranging from soft cuddly toys like teddy bears to bank robbery (hence the defence 'Straight up, your honour, I couldn't have kids of my own so I switched to doing banks'). A lot depends on which particular characteristics of the real child you wish to substitute for (e.g. cost, company, noise, smell, potential for grandchildren, etc). A wide selection of substitutes is outlined below:

- A dog: imposes similar demands to a child, and has the same slavish obedience and loyalty most children show up to the age of about seven. But dogs need a licence, which most children do not, and must wear a collar – which only some children do. One great advantage is that teenage dogs rarely compete for use of the bathroom.

- A cat: more independent than dogs and young kids, and doesn't need a licence. Good to have around, like a well-behaved child, but doesn't qualify you for child benefit.

- A knee in the groin: a good substitute for the agony and torment of finding the money to bring up a child. Less of a burden at holiday-time than a cat or a dog.

- A good hangover: a great substitute for the feeling of regret that often accompanies having children; the same 'Oh why did we do it?' feeling.

- A goldfish: has less interesting hobbies than a child, but is rarely the cause of broken nights. Also, goldfish are able to make you a great-great-great-great-great-great-great-great-great-grandparent in your own lifetime, which children cannot. However, it's not very easy to change a goldfish's nappy.

- A budgie: cheaper than a child, but more likely to fly away. Can't be relied upon to provide you with much comfort in your old age; more likely to crap on your hand instead. Again, fiddly when a nappy-change becomes necessary, but budgies rarely have any teething difficulties.

- A rhino: a good substitute for the mess and inconvenience of having a toddler around, but with greater novelty value. Not easy to get into a playgroup, and rather expensive to feed and dress.

- An Inspector of Taxes: a great substitute for the never-satisfied demands of the younger infant.

- A Bunny girl: a great substitute, at least as far as the father is concerned.

- A Porsche 928: an excellent substitute for practically anything, even a Bunny girl. If you can't have kids there is nothing better for cheering a parent up. Also can be left alone (if you can tear yourself away) for extended periods without crying. Almost never turns to delinquency.

- A bottle of gin: one of the few things that rivals a Porsche as a child substitute; may be beaten in the substitute stakes only by two bottles of gin.

- Open-heart surgery: has a very similar effect on life expectancy to that of a lively toddler. Is a good topic of conversation in the same way that kids are.

- An author: the ideal child substitute, in that authors are pleasant, entertaining, well-behaved, need a lot of support – especially financial – and appreciate good food.

'Higher, *Daddy!*'

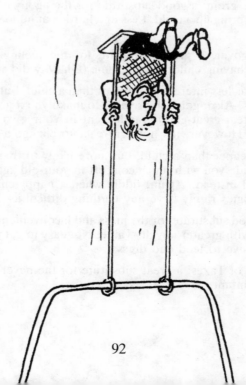

'Oh great, Dad . . . you've found my marble!'

'You just can't resist showing off in front of him, can you?'

A FINAL WORD

After I'd finished the manuscript for this book, I sat down and began to worry that I might have misrepresented the role of parenthood. Perhaps I'd exaggerated the problems, the crippling poverty, the mental stultification, the permanently ruined social life, the constant self-denial, the mental strain and worry, the disturbed nights, the premature ageing which result from having children. Perhaps my book would put people off having children altogether and herald the end of the human race as we know it. I pondered long and hard; in fact I pondered to the extent of about two bottles of gin. As I sank slowly into the mists of a pleasant alcoholic haze, my mind became clearer and the truth emerged from the fuddled mess of preconception, prejudice and short-sighted bigotry. Had I exaggerated the drawbacks? The truth was really quite simple.

I hadn't.